Move Over, Victoria— I Know the Real Secret!

Move Over, Victoria— I Know the Real Secret!

Surrendering the Lies That Bind You to the God Who Frees You

NANCY KENNEDY

WATERBROOK
PRESS

MOVE OVER, VICTORIA—I KNOW THE REAL SECRET!
PUBLISHED BY WATERBROOK PRESS
2375 Telstar Drive, Suite 160
Colorado Springs, Colorado 80920
A division of Random House, Inc.

Part of chapter 10, "Confessions of a Pro…crastinator," was adapted from my article
"Tomorrow's Another Day," in *Aspire,* August/September 1998.

All Scripture quotations, unless otherwise indicated, are taken from the *Holy Bible,*
New International Version®. NIV® Copyright © 1973, 1978, 1984 by the International
Bible Society. Used by permission of Zondervan Publishing House. All rights reserved.
Scripture quotations marked (TLB) are taken from *The Living Bible* copyright © 1971.
Used by permission of Tyndale House Publishers, Inc., Wheaton, Illinois 60189. All
rights reserved. Scripture quotations marked (MSG) are taken from *The Message.*
Copyright © by Eugene H. Peterson 1993, 1994, 1995. Used by permission of NavPress
Publishing Group. Scripture quotations marked (NASB) are taken from the *New American*
Standard Bible® (NASB). © Copyright The Lockman Foundation 1960, 1962, 1963, 1968,
1971, 1972, 1973, 1975, 1977. Used by permission. (www.Lockman.org) Scripture
quotations marked (CEV) are from the *Contemporary English Version.* Copyright © 1991,
1992, 1995 by American Bible Society. Used by permission. Scripture quotations marked
(KJV) are taken from the *King James Version.* Scripture quotations marked (AMP) are taken from
The Amplified Bible. Old Testament, copyright © 1965, 1987 by The Zondervan Corporation.
The Amplified New Testament, copyright © 1954, 1958, 1987 by The Lockman Foundation.
Used by permission.

ISBN 1-57856-200-7

Library of Congress Cataloging-in-Publication Data
Kennedy, Nancy, 1954–
    Move over, Victoria, I know the real secret! : surrendering the lies that bind you to the God
  who frees you / Nancy Kennedy.
        p. cm.
    ISBN 1-57856-200-7 (pbk.)
      1. Christian women—Religious life. 2. Idolatry. I. Title.
BV4527.K445 2000
248.8'43—dc21   00-033370

Printed in the United States of America
2001

10 9 8 7 6 5 4 3 2

This book is dedicated to
Alison, Laura, Peggy, and Jennifer.
Just because.

Contents

Contents

Foreword

There are three ingredients missing from most Christian books and almost all sermons. First, most Christian books and sermons aren't very honest. I don't mind being told how to be holy, what needs to be changed, or how to be better than I am. The problem is that there are very few experts in the field, and most who write and talk about those subjects write and talk as if their work came from Sinai. Now, if each sermon was preceded by a confession and each book with a chapter listing the author's sins, I would listen more closely and read more carefully. I might even change.

Second, most Christian books and sermons are so staid and serious that I can hardly get through them. (In fact, if you stand on them during a flood, you'll stay dry.) We take ourselves so *very* seriously. A monkey has a very serious look on his face, but the seriousness comes from fleas, not philosophy. If God is God and this is his show, if he loves us, and if he isn't a child abuser, we don't have to be so serious, so right, and so pure. If what we say we believe is true (and I have it on good authority that it is), then at least one appropriate reaction would be laughter…a free, joyous laughter from the only people who have anything to laugh about.

Third, most Christian books and sermons (especially if they do have honesty and humor) aren't very helpful. Frankly, I know a lot about God, the Bible, theology, and religion. Good heavens! I teach seminary students, write books, and preach sermons almost all the time. My problem is that I don't even come close to living up to the truth I already know. I need someone who has "dirt under his or her fingernails" to tell me something that will help, that will give me meaning…something that will make a difference in my life. I want to laugh with a preacher or a writer because life is hard. I want to be different after reading a book or listening to a sermon.

And that's why I like Nancy Kennedy's book. Nancy is incredibly honest, hilariously funny, and so practical and helpful that I honestly believe I can be different, can be free, and can turn from the "stuff" to a God who is quite fond of me.

I said at the beginning of this foreword that there were three ingredients missing from most Christian books and almost all sermons. Let me make a confession. Those same ingredients are often missing from my books and my sermons. Nancy Kennedy challenges me to be more honest, to laugh a bit more, and to be holy in the best sense of that word.

—STEVE BROWN, Key Life Network

Acknowledgments

Even though my name is on the cover, I'm not so naive as to think I could ever write a book alone. Although I'm not quite willing to share the royalties, I am more than happy to share the kudos, so here goes…

First of all, I owe a debt of gratitude to the following people:

Karen Pannella and Cindi Allen, friends who contributed more than they'll ever know to this book and to my life.

Ron Brown, my pastor-friend who gave me his (free!) counsel during the early stages of this book.

Jim Cole, my other pastor-friend and theological fact-checker—even on a Saturday.

Ray Cortese, my pastor (and friend, too) at Seven Rivers Presbyterian Church in Lecanto, whose material I steal liberally and regularly.

Barry and Laura, my extremely tolerant housemates. Thank you, Barry, for everything. I think I'll keep you another twenty-five years.

I also want to thank two people I've never met: Tim Keller, pastor of Redeemer Presbyterian Church in New York City, and the late Jack Miller, for their teachings on what it means to live as a child of God and to keep oneself from idols.

And thanks to Steve Brown, a totally cool dude.

A special note of gratitude to my team at WaterBrook Press: my editor, Traci Mullins; Erin Healy; Dan Rich; the sales representatives; and everyone else. What a pleasure working with you.

I'd say I idolize every one of you, but that would defeat the purpose of this book. Instead, I'll pray that each of you, "being rooted and established in love, may have power, together with all the saints, to grasp how wide and long and high and deep is the love of Christ, and to know this love that surpasses knowledge—that you may be filled to the measure of all the fullness of God" (Ephesians 3:17-19). Amen.

Dear children, keep yourselves from idols.
(1 John 5:21)

A Whale of a Predicament

If you could have three wishes, what would they be? To be rich? Famous? Gorgeous? What about happy? Now there's a generic wish. You might luck out and get riches *and* fame *and* beauty *and* happiness all in one wish and still have two more left. Then you could wish for a date with Brad Pitt or Sean Connery, plus a year's supply of chocolate-covered toffee. You could wish for world peace. Or that your kids would get along and never forget to make their beds and always remember to put their dirty underwear in the laundry hamper instead of stuffing it back in their dresser drawers. You could wish that God would answer your prayers the way you think he should or that the people around you would finally realize that your way *is* the best way to do things. You could wish for ten more wishes.

If I had three wishes, first I'd wish I were pretty. (Meg Ryan's face and Cindy Crawford's body would do nicely. Or even Cindy's face on Meg's body. I'm not particular.) Next I'd wish for enough money to buy a new car, pay off all my debts, and take a yearlong road trip around the United States with my husband. Then for my last wish…I'd wish I were free.

Not free as in "Oh goody, now I can do whatever I want," but rather free to be who God created me to be. Free to live like the much-loved child that I am. Free to consistently feel like a beloved daughter instead of a rag-clutching orphan. Free from thinking there's something more I could do or be in order to please my Father. Free of the guilt I still sometimes feel and of the fear that drives me away from God's throne of grace. Free to dance, to sing, to worship, to laugh.

Actually, I am free because Christ has set me free. But sometimes I don't live like I am. Do you ever feel that way too? You know in your head that Jesus is the answer to all your needs, but then you have a fight with your husband…and suddenly that Oreo cheesecake in the fridge looks mighty tasty. You're not hungry, but you're just so ticked you can't see straight. So you eat the whole thing. Then you're mad at yourself! (And you're certain God's mad too.) You think, *If only I could get to that place where I don't turn to food, but to Jesus!* And you feel even worse than before because you know you're not there.

Or maybe you're invited to a women's retreat and you want to go…but you don't have anything to wear and you think you'll feel out of place and conspicuous so you stay home. You want people to like you. You want to fit in. You want God to be pleased with you. *You want chocolate.* Or just one more pair of black shoes.

And you wish things were different. You wish you weren't so uptight about wanting your house (or hair or kids) to look as nice as your friend Brenda's, and you wish you didn't always say yes to everything. You wish you were a better wife, a better mom, a better friend. You wish you could control your temper—control everything, for that matter.

You wish you could be free of all that, once and for all. (See, I knew we had something in common!) You wish you could be free to love God and your family and your friends. Free to *be* loved. Free to eat corn on the cob in public without worrying about it getting caught in your teeth and causing certain death by embarrassment. Free to let go of all the things that hold you back or down or captive.

THEN ALONG CAME A FISH

I want to tell you about someone who found freedom from his trappings, not to mention a whopping dose of grace while in a most unusual place. You could say Jonah was in a whale of a predicament.

In case you're not familiar with his underwater adventure, Jonah was the Old Testament prophet whom God told to go one way but who decided instead to go in the opposite direction, taking an ocean cruise to flee from the Lord (Jonah 1:3). Since God frowns on such behavior, he sent a storm to rock Jonah's boat, so to speak. The crew members ended up tossing Jonah overboard, which calmed the raging sea but left the prophet sputtering seawater and looking for a life preserver.

Then along came a fish. One gulp and Jonah gave a whole new meaning to the word *seafood*. He spent the next three days and nights as some barracuda's breakfast.

I want you to pay close attention to what comes next: "From inside the fish Jonah prayed" (Jonah 2:1). Isn't that wild? I mean, if you've just been swallowed by a huge fish, what else are you going to do? But really look at Jonah's prayer for a minute. It wasn't entirely one of distress. He didn't whine and moan and complain about his accommodations. Instead, he acknowledged that it was God who placed him in a fish belly (v. 3). Then, with seaweed wrapped around his head, he expressed gratitude to the Lord for bringing his life up from the pit (v. 6). (Remember, he was still inside the fish when he prayed this—and with no secret escape hatch or emergency exit in sight!) He said, "When my life was ebbing away, I remembered you, LORD, and my prayer rose to you, to your holy temple" (v. 7). From inside the belly of a fish, knowing he's fish bait, Jonah gave praise to the Lord. Don'tcha love it?

He also said something that has haunted me for years: "Those who cling to worthless idols forfeit the grace that could be theirs" (v. 8). It doesn't say what those idols were or whose they were, but if you ask me, if I'm the one treading water inside some flounder, the only idols I'd be thinking about would be my own. I guess when you're inside a fish you have lots of time to think, and maybe thinking about worthless idols is as good as anything.

Here's my personal theory on Jonah's situation, and everyone else's: We hold on to things (we cling to "worthless idols"), seeking comfort, affirmation, self-worth, and love from them because we don't truly know who God is. Before we know it, we're trapped.

I'm trapped when I seek approval from others, forgetting that God is the one true Lover of my soul, the One who takes great delight in me and rejoices over me with singing (Zephaniah 3:17). I'm trapped when I buy yet one more pink T-shirt to add to my already-stuffed closet, forgetting that God has clothed me with Christ himself (Galatians 3:27). The list goes on, but I can't tell you everything in the introduction! I'll just have to be patient and wait.

I'll give you a little hint though. The main point I want to make in the pages ahead is that knowing God sets us free and enables us to let go of the things we cling to *because he is so much greater*. That's what Jonah realized deep in the belly of that fish. That's what we need to realize too. You think this over, and we'll talk later. For now, let me tell you about my friend Karen Pannella.

Karen carries around a notebook in which she keeps a list of God's attributes. Each week she writes down a different aspect of his nature and the scriptures associated with that particular trait. Then she keeps track of how the Lord reveals himself to her in that way throughout the week.

I'm not that organized, but I benefit from Karen's hard work. When she and I meet every week to pray, she reads me what she has written in her notebook and then we pray together, concentrating on that one facet of the infinite Almighty. You really should join us sometime because it's *awesome* when we're able to see the way God humbles himself from upon his throne in heaven to show us who he is and how he is more than able (and oh so willing) to meet our deepest needs.

So I've been thinking… If knowing God enables me to rid myself of the things that hold me and if he frees me to experience the lavishness of his glorious grace, then that's what I want. To know him truly, deeply, experientially. To know that I know that I know. To be so filled with the knowledge of him that I'd gladly cast aside anything standing in my way. I want that for you, too.

Sound scary? It scares me until I remember that no matter what we're holding on to, God still loves us and wants us to know it. As author, Bible teacher, and all-around neat guy Steve Brown likes to point out, God is quite fond of us and isn't mad anymore if we are his.

Oh my! I've got so much to tell you. I hope you're as excited as I am to get started. I'll just close by saying I've prayed for you, that you will find hope and encouragement and laughter as we discuss both the things that hold us and the awesome God who sets us free. I've included some thoughts to ponder at the end of each chapter, along with some questions to ask yourself or maybe discuss with a friend or small group. I encourage you to get into the Bible for yourself. While I'm tickled that you bought this book, only God's Word contains the truth to transform your life. Use the questions I've provided to dig deep and mine the precious nuggets of Scripture. You'll be glad you did.

By the time you finish this book, I pray you'll have discovered God in ways you've never considered before (or have tended to forget). Maybe you'll even be able to let go of the things you so desperately cling to and find the freedom God promises you in Christ. After all, that's what we've wished for, right?

Chapter 1

Idol Chatter

The art of pressing flowers is as relevant today as it was one hundred years ago.—Martha Stewart

If I tell you something, promise you won't laugh? *I love Martha Stewart.* From her edible flower salads to her monogrammed garden work gloves, I love her. Everything she does exceeds any superlative my puny mortal brain could devise. She's...otherworldly. She's stare-with-your-mouth-open astounding. She makes life-size gingerbread doghouses and grows her own potatoes. She does everything with perfection.

She makes her own marshmallows.

I go about my day wondering *WWMD?* (What would Martha do?). My ears perk up when I hear her name. My face lights up when I speak about her. I love her magazine; I love her television show. I even love her This-is-how-*I*-make-a-bed video that plays nonstop in the linen section of Kmart. ("All Martha, all the time.") It's a good thing, you know.

My family thinks I'm obsessed, but I'm *not.* I'm simply...pursuing all I can about the art of domesticity. On the other hand, maybe my family is right.

You see, like you, my heart has a need to worship. It's what I was created for. I know God is the One who deserves my worship, and I want to worship only him, but there's a problem. Something always seems to come along to entice me, to grab my attention and steal my affection. There's a tug of war inside me, pulling me in a million directions, away from God and toward other, lesser things. If it's not Martha Stewart, it's e-mail or Mel Gibson. It's Rush Limbaugh, the newest dollar store, or my must-have bowl of Frosted Flakes in the afternoon. The Bible calls such things "idols." "Worthless idols."

I don't know about you, but I'm not too crazy about the idea of idolatry, especially if that idolatry is mine. I don't like to think of myself as an idolater. Idol worshipers are ancient pagans who sacrifice virgins and bow down to statues. They conduct rituals until God gets mad and smites them or sends plagues to wipe them out. But that's not me! I'm a suburban, American, church-going, tax-paying, Bible-reading Christian. I don't have any idols…or do I?

The truth? I do have them—lots of them—if you consider an idol to be any thing, person, place, idea, substance, or activity that I turn to *first*, before God, for comfort, pleasure, satisfaction, purpose, or meaning in life. It's something that I think I can't live without. You know, like chocolate.

HAND OVER THE SNICKERS AND NO ONE WILL GET HURT!

I'll never forget the time a friend of mine confronted me during a break at our church's women's retreat. As I madly rifled through my purse for my bag of emergency chocolate (my motto being "You never know when you'll be in a situation without a vending machine nearby") and then bit into a milk-chocolate-covered maple crème, my eyes rolled back from the ecstasy of the chocolate rush. *Ahhhhh.* It was on my second bite that my friend shook her head in obvious disdain and blurted out, "Nancy, chocolate is your god!"

I laughed, but her words stung. I told her she was wrong. That I could quit anytime I wanted. Then I went back to my room and cried. Sobbed as if someone had taken my dog out back and shot him. Truly there has never been a more pathetic creature than I, clutching my stash of chocolate bliss and letting the tears roll down my face.

Once I had composed myself, I briefly toyed with the notion that just maybe there was a slight possibility that perhaps what my friend had said was somewhat semitruthful. *She had accused me of being an idolater.* A worshiper of cocoa, fat, and sugar.

Earlier the retreat speaker had asked, "What holds you? What is your greatest passion? What's the first thing you think about when you get up in the morning and the last thing at night? What motivates you? Captures your attention? Grabs your heart?"

I knew the correct answer was, of course, Jesus. But I also knew the honest answer—my honest answer—was *not* Jesus. At that moment my greatest passion was in a plastic bag inside my purse. It's what I had wanted *first.*

I squirmed and wiggled as the speaker continued her talk (and I continued thinking about Hershey's Kisses and Whitman's Samplers). Then, of all things, I thought about Jonah and what he had prayed while he was inside the belly of that fish and about worthless idols and forfeited grace. I'd never thought of myself as an idol worshiper before, but that's exactly what my friend had called me.

I wish I could tell you that confrontation was my moment of epiphany, of radical repentance, of falling on my face and "throw[ing] off everything that hinders and the sin that so easily entangles" (Hebrews 12:1). Instead, it was a moment of defensiveness…and anger.

How dare she tell me chocolate is my god! Who does she think she is? Then my anger turned to fear. *What if I had to give it up? I couldn't do it! The agony would be too much for me.* I even felt despondent. *If I can't eat chocolate, what reason would there be to continue living?*

Well, maybe that's being a tad melodramatic. I probably wouldn't die if I couldn't eat chocolate, but I'd be awfully cranky.

I decided right then and there to do what I usually do when confronted with a difficult decision or circumstance. I tried to ignore it, hoping the whole subject of idolatry would go away. Besides, it's such a negative concept. Idol worship is what *sinners* do.

So you can clearly see why I took offense to my friend's words and why I tried to push the whole subject out of my mind. But you know how God is. (Or if you don't, I'll tell you: When he wants to reveal something in your life, he's as relentlessly persistent as a teenage daughter who wants a tattoo.)

I don't remember exactly how it happened, but God did what God does best. Just when I thought I'd found a loophole ("Idolatry is something ancient Bible characters were guilty of, and besides, *I'm* under grace"), I remembered that God is still God and still says he'll have no other gods before him. That includes chocolate. Now, I'm not saying chocolate is bad or it's a sin to eat or enjoy it. However, if I feel I must carry around a bag of it in case of an emergency, there's a problem.

As I said, I don't remember how it happened. If I'd had a lightning-bolt experience where you shout "Hallelujah!" and gather up all the chocolate you have stashed, set it on fire, and never eat another tasty morsel again, I would've remembered. But I think I just repented. Acknowledged that chocolate was too important in my life. That I turned to it before I turned to my Father. That I needed to know him better.

As it is, I still eat chocolate, but I don't carry around an emergency stash anymore. Something has changed inside. Now before you start thinking I've conquered the area of idolatry in my life, be assured that I have not. But I'm learning, s-l-o-w-l-y, that the sweetness I've sought in chocolate (and so many other things) can only be found in the sweetness of God's love.

GRACE FORFEITERS

If your experience of life is anything like mine, something is always trying to lure you away from the grace of God. Not from his saving grace, but from the experience of it, the walking in the knowledge of his pleasure. These so-called worthless idols grab your affection and tell you lies. They promise love and power, comfort and pleasure, but fail to deliver. Before you realize that, however, you willingly "forfeit the grace that could be yours" and end up feeling emptier than before.

What has you forfeiting your grace? What holds you? Captures your attention and your heart? Has you bound up and yearning to be free?

Tim Keller, Bible teacher and pastor of Redeemer Presbyterian Church in Manhattan, offers this test for identifying idols in your life. In his study of Galatians he asks: Is there something *too* important to you? Is there a person, experience, possession, position, relationship, etc. that if you can't have it, you get (excessively) angry, fearful, badly worried, or despondent?

- If you are angry, ask yourself: What is it that I think I *have* to have that I'm being blocked from obtaining or achieving?

- If you are fearful or worried: What is it that I think I *have* to have that I feel is being threatened?

- If you are feeling despondent: What is it that I think I *have* to have that I've either lost or failed at?[1]

As for me, I'm not generally prone to anger and I'm almost never despondent. I am, however, often fearful. I'm afraid that one day we won't be able to pay our bills and the bank will repossess our house. (I'm held by the need for security.) I'm afraid that if I don't do something—anything—nothing good will happen, and everyone I love will make wrong decisions and destroy themselves and me along with them. Or at least make me cry. (I'm held by the need to control.)

The need for approval and acceptance also holds my heart. I'm afraid of standing alone for Christ when everyone around me, even family members, ridicules my beliefs. I'm afraid of people who talk behind other people's backs. Afraid that if I'm too odd they'll talk behind mine. I'm terrified of making unpopular parental decisions.

I'm also afraid to let people close. I keep them at arm's length. (I'm held by the desire for independence and self-reliance.) My daughters always accuse me of "interviewing" people—asking a thousand questions, yet rarely offering anything of myself. I tell myself that I'm trying to be a good listener or that I'm "esteeming others more highly than myself," as the Bible says, but the truth is I'm scared of letting people in.

Martin Luther once said, "Whatever your heart clings to and relies upon, that is your God." Even before that, from inside a fish, Jonah said that the things that hold us, the idols in our lives, are, in essence, grace for-feiters, grace stealers.

I know all about that. A long time ago I almost had God's grace sucked right out of me. Theologically, I know that's not possible. Once God extends his saving grace to a person, he never removes it or snatches it away. We, however, can turn up our noses at it and allow something else to steal away our affection, forfeiting the benefits of his grace. At any rate, I once felt as if all grace was gone from my life.

I'm embarrassed and ashamed to tell you this, but I instigated and par-ticipated in a forbidden flirtation with a man who was not my husband. It was all one-sided on my part—I don't think the man had a clue as to my feelings toward him. But God did.

Eventually this other person occupied all my waking thoughts and even my dreams. I felt dirty and yucky, but I couldn't seem to change. The truth is, I didn't want to. So I allowed this worthless idol in my life to continue robbing me of the grace that could've been mine as I clung to it with all my might.

WHEN YOU COME TO A FORK IN THE ROAD, TAKE IT

This is what happens: My clinging to idols becomes reciprocal. I cling to something, hoping it will satisfy whatever it is in me that needs satisfying, and it does…at first. But then something shifts, and the thing I'm holding on to begins to hold on to me.

In the case of my one-sided love affair, it had me so bound that at times

I couldn't even think clearly. Finally the Lord brought me to a fork in the road where I had to make a choice: I could continue clinging to my idol, living a happily-ever-after fantasy existence that displeased God and rendered me useless in his kingdom because of my feelings of guilt and shame, or I could choose freedom.

Friend, this might not sound like a big deal, but it was by far one of the hardest choices I've ever had to make. I'm not telling you this simply as an illustration either; it goes far deeper than that. This was a pivotal experience in my life, a time when I "got it." *It* being the knowledge of the depth of my sin in comparison to the greatness of God's gift of salvation and the abundant life he offers to his children. I truly, completely, totally understood Jonah's words, "Those who cling to worthless idols forfeit the grace that could be theirs." I'd known what it was to cling and what it was to feel as if God had turned his back on me.

I won't go into details except to tell you I unclenched my fist and made the necessary adjustments in my life to remove myself from the grip of this idol. As I did, it was as if the windows of heaven opened and grace rained down on me. "Free from guilt, his blood has washed [me]," as a favorite hymn says. I still suffered the grief involved with ending a relationship (albeit a one-sided, secret one), but I got my life back.

Then, shortly after that, I went through one of the darkest periods of my life, as if I'd provoked an unseen enemy (which I had). It seemed obedience to God had removed me from Satan's Benign Christians List, and I guess that ticked the enemy off. However, the grace I had once forfeited became my strength, and I vowed never to let anything other than God hold me ever again.

Unfortunately, my vows are as worthless as…well, as yours are, because it seems every time I turn around I'm flirting with something else. I suspect you're the same way. *But God wants to give us grace.* He wants us to open our hands in surrender and worship to him and be free. Free to be who we were created to be: much-loved, eternally secure children who worship the one true God.

It all comes down to this: Whom shall I serve, God or myself? Everything that seeks to steal me away from experiencing the freedom of God's grace points to self: *my* comfort, *my* image, *my* reputation, *my* desire to control other people and my surroundings. The problem is not chocolate; it's the importance I place on the pleasure that chocolate brings. It's not Martha Stewart; it's the idea that if I follow her example, people will adore me, too.

WHAT PART OF THE GOSPEL AREN'T YOU BELIEVING?

My friend Cindi has a favorite question. Whenever she sees that I'm flirting with a worthless idol, she asks me a pointed question: "What part of the gospel aren't you believing?" In other words, what aspect of God's nature am I doubting? His unwavering love for me? His willingness to forgive? His ever-sufficient grace? His power, truth, glory, and majesty? To be honest, at times I doubt all the above.

I think it's because secretly I want to *be* God. Oh, I wouldn't ever come right out and say that out loud. I'd rather die than have you think of me as being that presumptuous and arrogant! But you know what? Sometimes I think I know better than God how my life should go. Besides, he's in his holy heaven somewhere out there taking care of wars and famines and floods and probably could use a break. He might even appreciate my taking over every once in a while.

Plus, I want to help. And be his instrument in answering my own prayers. I want to feel good about the things I do for him. I want him to peer down from his throne and point me out to all the angels and say, "See my servant Nancy? Did you notice the way she faithfully sits on the front row at church each week and dutifully takes notes during her pastor's sermons? Did you see the way she volunteered once for nursery duty and read the entire book of Galatians at one sitting? Did you take note of how she set her timer last week and stayed on her knees praying for twelve whole minutes (without getting up to check her e-mail *even* when it chimed, 'You've got mail!')?"

The struggle with idols boils down to this: God is God and I am not. But I want to be. It's the Garden of Eden all over again, when the serpent offered Adam and Eve the opportunity to "be like God" (Genesis 3:5) and they swallowed the lie. Ever since, Eve's sons and daughters have fallen for the same line. But because God is who he is, he has a *gospel,* literally, "good news." He says to his creation, You're evil through and through. Totally depraved—bad to the bone. But I love you! "I have loved you with an everlasting love; I have drawn you with loving-kindness" (Jeremiah 31:3).

The catch is, although he loves us, he still requires perfection—and we've already blown it. But because he loves us, he has provided a way for us to be right with him. The Father sent the Son to live the perfect life we never could and then to die the perfect death, both living and dying in our place. Then he rose from death to prove himself almighty. All he requires from us is to humbly repent of our trying to be God, receive his gift of life through faith, and rejoice forever because he takes delight in us and has good things planned for our lives.

Sounds simple if you ask me. Unfortunately, I don't like simple. I want to *do* something, do my part. It's not enough that God has done it all. The part of me that wants to "help" is still alive and well. I'm still an idolater. I still turn to anything and everything other than God alone.

I still want to be God!

But I'm not. However, the more I get to know him and who he really is, and the more I realize I've done my part by simply being a sinner in need of salvation, and the more I see myself as being even worse than I ever thought possible, the more willing I am to see that his grace is greater than I could ever imagine. The more I know him, the greater is my trust that he does know best and that his love for me is a sure bet. To know him is to love him. To love him is to trust him. To trust him is to find freedom to serve him, not out of a sense of duty, but out of sheer gratitude.

So with the words of the apostle Paul, "I ask the glorious Father and God of our Lord Jesus Christ to give [us] his Spirit. The Spirit will make [us] wise and let [us] understand what it means to know God" (Ephesians 1:17, CEV). Because to know him, as Martha Stewart would say, is a good thing.

A *very* good thing.

Think on These Things

1. What are some ways people react when they lose something precious or want something they can't have? How do you react?

2. What are some of the false promises and lies of idols? What reasons do people give for not wanting to let go of them?

3. What are some of the idols in your life? Use the following questions to help you identify them:

    What is your greatest fear/worry?

    What do you turn to *first* for comfort?

    What accomplishment, possession, or relationship makes you feel the greatest sense of self-worth?

What occupies your thinking? Where does your mind wander?

What unanswered prayer might cause you to doubt God to the point of turning away?

On what do you spend the majority of your time, energy, and money?

4. Read Galatians 1:1-10. How can idols in your life be compared to "turning to a different gospel"? What are the elements of the true gospel? (See 1 John 4:9-10; Romans 3:10-18; Romans 4:4-8; Romans 11:5-6; Romans 10:9-10; Romans 8:1-2; Galatians 5:1.)

Prone to wander, Lord, I feel it,
Prone to leave the God I love;
Here's my heart, O, take and seal it;
Seal it for Thy courts above.

—Robert Robinson, "Come, Thou Fount of Every Blessing"

Chapter 2

The Empress Isn't Wearing Any Clothes!

If I'm going to be a hypocrite, at least I want to look cute.—Cathy

You're going to find out sooner or later, so I might as well tell you now: I'm not who you think I am. I'm not even sure if I'm who I think I am. See, I think I'm this easygoing, mild-mannered, exceptionally warm and loving woman. I think I'm in my mid-twenties (I'm forty-five), short (that, I am), and a great friend to all, including stray animals. (I haven't called my own mother in months, and I told my neighbor's dumb white bird to go lay an egg when it spit at me the other day.)

I think of myself as witty and charming. Someone who should be photographed in rolled-up white pants and an off-the-shoulder white sweater on a beach somewhere as the ocean breeze blows my long, flowing blond tresses across my face. (I have short, spiky brown hair that I keep plastered with hair spray, thus maintaining a perpetual helmet head that wouldn't budge in a hurricane.)

In my own eyes, I am wise and generous. Bright and caring, a paragon of Christian virtue. A kick in the pants. A hoot and a half. Mary Poppins and Julia Roberts rolled into one. I am, as the teenagers say, *all that.* That's how I see myself…in my dreams. Then I roll out of bed, pull on a pair of shorts and a faded T-shirt, and sit at my computer screen scratching my armpits while desperately trying to maintain the illusion of a Put-Together Woman. I'm pretty good at faking it, as long as I don't have to go out of the house.

"MIRROR, MIRROR ON THE WALL… CAN'T YOU DO SOMETHING?"

Recently I attended a Christian business convention. There were men in suits and women in scarves and big jewelry and shoes other than scuffed-up Reeboks. Not a faded T-shirt on the whole convention floor. Just wall-to-wall professional types, some high-profile Christian celebrities…and me. It's enough to make an insecure person like me want to fade into the floor tiles.

While at this convention, I had an epiphany moment, which I'll tell you about later. I like to save the good stuff for last. First I'll tell you about the week before the convention as I spent nearly every day staring into my packed closet, bemoaning the fact that I had nothing to wear.

But it was more than that. Even in my best clothes, I knew I still wouldn't be dressed right. I wouldn't project the right image. I don't do scarves, and silk blouses make me sweat. I buy my clothes at bargain outlets. I always forget to wear a pin on the lapel of my jacket. I thought everyone there would surely realize that I'm an impostor. After all, if I don't look like a Professional Christian, how effective could I be? I knew that image is a big part of business, and I obviously didn't have It. Although I'm still not sure what It is, I just knew that I wanted It—and I was determined to find It.

So I went to the mall.

It was as if God knew I was coming. As I walked through the department store door, a young woman, looking eager in her white lab coat, approached me and offered me a free cosmetics makeover and style consultation. I'm normally skeptical of such things, but I saw this as a sign. Besides, I'm a sucker for anything free.

It must've been her first day on the job or else she missed the lesson on discernment and accurate analysis because she insisted that my style was "casual/funky." Never on my best day have I been described as "funky," but she was young and I was desperate.

As she worked on my face, she rattled off all the essentials I'd need to build my casual-slash-funky wardrobe. "You'll need to pair a sleek pantsuit with a great pair of chunky loafers or high-heeled boots," she told me.

Sleek is for jaguars, sweetie, I thought, *and not for a pear-shaped size fourteen petite like me.*

"Of course you'll want to invest in a good leather biker jacket—that's *pivotal.*"

I'm forty-five and having hot flashes.

"Maybe a fitted, button-down shirt or chunky sweater with a long, clingy animal-skin print skirt."

Any sweater on me automatically becomes "chunky." As for the clingy skirt, obviously you haven't seen my thighs.

"Oh, and make sure your pants have a flat front and a slight flare at the bottom."

Again, sweetie, you assume too much. I've never had a flat front, although I do have a bottom that's naturally flared.

Then, with the naiveté of youth, she announced that I should definitely indulge in a "decadent" velvet bustier or a push-up bra. "Thong panties," she added, "are a given."

Well, if that's true, I thought, *then I'm giving them back.* Actually, the bustier didn't sound too terribly ridiculous. I wondered if they made an orthopedic model for a woman my age.

After another few minutes of her theories about strategic accessorizing ("I always say, you can't go wrong with four or five simple earrings in each ear and a chain choker around your neck"), she finished painting my lips with a red the color of liver and handed me a mirror.

I looked...funky. But inside I was still a raving middle-aged mother of two. Not a funky bone in my body. Born to barbecue, not to boogie.

I declined her services as a personal shopper and instead thanked her for her time and dashed off to the nearest bathroom to scrub all the gook off my face. Funk down the drain. As for what I wore to the convention, I ended up wearing something from the back of my closet and lipstick the color of lips, not liver. It wasn't It, but it had to do.

SMILE AND SAY, "PLEASE GOD, DON'T LET THIS LOOK LIKE ME!"

In forty-five years, I've only had two photos of myself that didn't make me want to either cry or puke—or do both. The best one is of me at about six months of age, bare-bottomed on a white fur rug, clutching a rubber ducky, my hair swirled into a Kewpie doll curl on the top of my head. If I do say so myself, I was the cutest thing you'll ever see…and I've been trying to maintain that image ever since.

The other photo was taken about six years ago after I wrote my first book and needed a publicity photo. (The publisher wouldn't accept the rubber ducky pose.) In this photo I'm sitting in a white wicker chair, wearing my favorite aqua three-dollar sweater. At the time I bought a bunch of copies, but after six years, I have only one left. That isn't a problem, since I don't normally go around handing out my picture to strangers on the street. However, recently someone requested a photo to accompany a magazine article I had written.

Here's the dilemma: Do I send the one and only photo of myself (six years younger and ten pounds lighter) that I actually like, or have a new one taken that more accurately reflects the added weight and years? To say the whole issue caused great inner turmoil and emotional distress would be akin to saying Mel Gibson looks "okay" in a kilt. Nothing gives me greater agony than having my picture taken. The problem is, I'm terrified it will turn out to look just like me. There's nothing worse than a dose of reality to knock you on your keister.

I remember being self-conscious as a child to the point of obsession about my Fatal Flaws (as I called them)—large nose, thin lips, no chin, and perpetual acne. My dad used to tease and say, "Cheer up! No one's going to look at you anyway." He was right, you know. That's because everyone's too busy obsessing over his or her own Fatal Flaws to notice mine. None of us is ever really satisfied with just being who God created us to be.

After much inner debate, I decided I needed to get another photo done and called around for a photographer with supernatural abilities to make me look, if not good, at least not so bad. That's my goal now, to look Not So Bad.

I wore my same aqua three-dollar sweater, same hairstyle and makeup, same earrings. I had hoped to recreate the same photo I'd had taken six years earlier. I prayed for a miracle and begged God to be merciful to me, a puffy-faced sinner.

The good news is, God is always merciful. The bad news is, the photo looks just like me—and I just don't like the way I look. The real me doesn't fit the image of the me inside my head. Or, maybe the real me truly is Not So Bad. After all, I've yet to scare anyone away.

"WHAT WILL PEOPLE THINK?"

If I had to narrow it down to one phrase to describe my life it would have to be, "What will people think?" While it's true that I spend an inordinate amount of time worrying about my appearance, I spend more time trying to appear "good." I want people to think of me as a good person, a good wife and mom, a good friend and church member, a good employee. Of course, I want to actually be all these things, but if I'm honest, sometimes it's more important that I merely look as if I am. I think, *If I get the externals right, maybe the internals will follow. If I look good, maybe I'll eventually be good. Or, if I look good, it doesn't matter if I am good, as long as other people think I am.*

Not only that, sometimes I think God expects me to look good in order to maintain a spotless Christian image. As if I'm somehow defending his image with my own. It then becomes my responsibility, my duty, to look as good as I can. It matters what other people think, or so I think. Sometimes it matters even more than what God thinks—and it holds me captive.

ALONG COMES A FISH...

One of the things I like most about God is his sense of irony. The minute you tell him you wouldn't be caught dead doing *whatever*, you can pretty much bet that's what you'll be doing someday. He knows the right buttons to push. Or he knows we need a fish, as in Jonah's case, to get our attention.

I'm going to let you in on one of my deepest, darkest secrets. More than anything else, I want people to think I'm a good mom. Did you catch that? I want people to *think* I'm a good mom. Of course I want to be one, but I have a hunch that I'm not. So the next best thing is presenting the Good Mom image.

If you ever meet my older daughter, Alison, you will immediately think, "Wow, her mom must surely be a Good Mom." At twenty-three, Alison is polite, sweet, loyal, thrifty, and all those other Girl Scout–type superlatives. She makes me look good. Yea, Alison! Give her a cookie!

And then there's Laura.

Don't get me wrong. She is the delight of my life, and in many ways I admire her greatly. She's opinionated and unafraid to say what she thinks. She's the baby I begged God for. But...currently, at age sixteen, she's into wearing black. Big black platform Mary Janes and long black skirts. Short black dresses and black bump-toed combat boots. Black hair. Several assorted holes in her ears...and a silver stud on the side of her nose. She's..."out there." Her friends, too, are "out there." They have hair the color of Skittles and pointy things sticking out of their faces. They wear dog collars and plaid pants. They're the type of kids who, as soon as you take one look at them, you *know* their moms can't possibly be Good Moms because a Good Mom would *never* have a kid who looked like that!

And my kid looks like that.

But I also know that my daughter and her current friends are, for the most part, nice kids—and that some of the "normal" looking kids she knows aren't so nice. You can't always judge by externals…yet I worry, *What will people think?*

WHAT DOES *GOD* THINK?

When it comes to our appearance, the color of our eyes, the shape of our noses, the size of our earlobes, we may worry and fret, moan and cry, but God thinks we're just fine the way he made us. "Fearfully and wonderfully made," as the psalm goes (Psalm 139:14). However, for someone obsessed with her appearance, whether seeking beauty she never had or holding on to looks that are fading, those words sound too simplistic.

I have a friend who admitted to me in a letter, "I can't help it! I spend money I don't have on haircuts I can't afford; I'm always at the mall buying new clothes; I bleach my teeth; I get body wraps and now I want facials. I think I'm addicted to myself. My boss calls me Mrs. Vain, but I'm NOT. It's all a cover-up. I used to want to be happy, but I've given up on that. Now all I want is to look good."

What should I tell her? God loves you, stop worrying, snap out of it, get a life? How can knowing that the Lord of creation decided to make her five foot six with size-seven feet and a spray of freckles across her nose help her stop being obsessed with her looks? What does God think about my friend and about me?

The real answer is the hard answer, the painful answer. As with everything that holds us, we first have to come to see our obsessions and preoccupations for what they are—idols. Our image is our god, and the real God says he will have no other gods before him. Therefore, we are in sin. (I tried to make that sound nicer, but sometimes truth isn't nice.)

Truth is freeing, however. Although it's rarely pleasant, I've come to value the times when I'm confronted with my sin. Sounds crazy, I know, but I experience the joy of God's forgiveness only when I admit my sin. I have to call it that and nothing less. When I confess my sin, not only is he faithful and just to forgive me, but also to purify me from all unrighteousness (1 John 1:9). Now that's good news!

When it comes to idols such as my image, the only way to get them to loosen their hold on me is to *repent, replace,* and *rejoice.*

- Repent by:
  1. Naming the idol specifically. ("My image is too important to me. It is taking a wrongful place in my thoughts and heart, the place where only God belongs.")
  2. Unmasking its power. ("God has created me to find satisfaction in him alone. Beauty is fleeting; image is only external. Neither reflects who I really am.")
  3. Identifying the lie and its danger. ("I thought if I could look a certain way other people—even God—would accept me. If I continue chasing after the perfect image, I'll end up alienating myself from the only One who matters, my Creator.")

- Replace by:
  Substituting Christ. Search the Scriptures and preach the gospel to yourself until you believe it in its entirety, until you're convinced that Jesus is enough.

- Rejoice by:
  Seeking the heart of God until the part of you that is tempted to seek elsewhere finds satisfaction, and thanking him for his loving-kindness toward you.

This isn't a magic formula that comes with a money-back guarantee if you're not completely free in thirty days. Rather, it's a process, often a life-long process, that requires diligence and perseverance.

Remember I told you about having an epiphany moment at the convention? It occurred the day I brought Laura with me. There we were on the convention floor, me in my conservative bargain suit and Battenberg lace blouse, walking with my Goth Princess daughter dressed in black. (Before you get a wrong mental picture of her, let me assure you she's cute as a button and not into hideous black makeup and outrageous clothes. But she is noticeable.)

As we walked through the crowds, I was acutely aware of two things. First, that we were attracting stares. But more important, that I was simply overjoyed to have my daughter with me. Sure, her sense of style is bizarre, but for right now that's who she is—*and she's my kid.* She's my kid, and I couldn't wait to introduce her to the people I had met at the convention.

That's when it hit me: That's how God sees all his kids! We try hard to present an image, put our best (or sometimes strangest) face forward—whether it be as a Professional, a Good Mom, a Weird Teenager, a Pretty Woman—and God sees past all that to who we really are. As long as we're in Christ, God looks at each one of us and says, "That's my kid. And despite all her flaws and imperfections, I love her!"

Is that enough to make me stop being consumed with wanting to look good and worrying about what people think of me? In theory, the answer is yes. In reality, it will take a lifetime of conscious decisions, of repenting, replacing, and rejoicing. The good news is, it gets easier with practice as I remember that the Lord is a Master Designer who never makes mistakes. He created me the way he wanted me—specifically, carefully, fearfully, and wonderfully.

What about other people? There will always be those who will judge me inaccurately. After all, people tend to think what they want to think, and some only want to think the worst. Others will decide I should be funky when I'm not or that a Good Mom should have a daughter in hair bows instead of combat boots. But the truth is, my Father loves me. And with the Creator's stamp of approval, really, what more do I need to be free?

Think on These Things

1. What do you think of when you hear the word *image?* What types of images do people try to project, and how do they go about achieving them?

2. Proverbs 31:30 says, "Charm is deceptive, and beauty is fleeting; but a woman who fears the LORD is to be praised." What is charm, and how is it deceptive? Name some of the lies or false expectations connected with the pursuit of one's image.

3. Read Genesis 1:1-31, the account of creation. What do you think it means to be created in God's image (v. 27)? Read and reflect on Psalm 139:13-18. List specific ways in which you are fearfully and wonderfully made.

4. Meditate on (or memorize!) Romans 12:1-2. How have you conformed "to the pattern of this world" by chasing after a personal image? Write out your confession as a prayer to the Lord, using the three *R* elements *(repent, replace, rejoice)*. Keep in mind that if you're afraid or reluctant to surrender your idols, God knows your heart and he loves you tenderly. All he wants is for you to be free indeed.

How can our self-image be low when we contemplate the image of God
in which we were created?... I feel best about myself, not when I am wearing
a new outfit, but when I have selflessly reached out to someone in need....
It is only when my self *is submerged that God's image begins to shine forth.*
Then I have a healthy self-image that truly reflects God's image.
—Ruth A. Tucker, *Women's Devotional Bible*

Chapter 3

Ring Dings and Twinkies and Fudge, Oh My!

My whole life revolves around dessert.—Marvin Hamlisch

How fondly I recall my first True Love. I called him Chip. As in, chip off the ol' block. Block of fudge, that is.

My mother had done the melted Nestlé morsel and Kraft marshmallow creme in a jar thing that was popular back in the *Leave It to Beaver* days, whipping it with her wire whisk over the double boiler on the stove, shooing me away as I kept sticking my face and grubby toddler paws into the bowl. I couldn't have been more than three, but even at that early age, I knew True Love when I tasted it. True Love was a hardened piece of chocolate fudge, broken up into little chips so I could have "lots" on my plate. *Tell me that isn't love.*

Ah, but that was before I discovered the magical, even medicinal, powers of anything made by Hostess. Snowballs—balls of snowy marshmallow. Cupcakes—delicate cups of chocolate cake, just big enough to fit in one's hand. Handy enough to shove into one's face any time, any place.

Whimsical Ring Dings and sturdy Suzy Q's. Just thinking about them stirs something within me.

As for Twinkies—truly God himself must have created them, for there has never been, nor ever will be, a more perfect food. Golden as the sun itself. A tri-squirting of whatever that white stuff is. (Could the three holes be further evidence of the Holy Trinity?) Even the layer of Twinkie cake residue that sticks to the cardboard when you take it out of the package and that you scrape off with your finger is a deliciously added bonus that *only* could have been placed there by a loving God.

Yet, as indisputably perfect as Twinkies might be, sometimes not even a mouthful of heavenly sponge cake and cream satisfies the deepest yearnings of the soul. For true satisfaction and ultimate bliss—nirvana, if you will— nothing beats the surpassing power of chocolate. I told you earlier that I liked, even loved, chocolate, but I held back on telling you just how much I loved it. I thought I'd wait until now to sing its praises.

Have a bad day? Chocolate comforts like no other substance or force on earth. (There's a reason why Hershey's calls its candies Kisses and Hugs.) Have a fight with your husband? Break up with your boyfriend? Chocolate not only understands, but loves you unconditionally and stays with you forever…on your hips. *What a friend I have in chocolate! Chocolate, chocolate, how I love thee! Chocolate is all the world to me, my life, my joy, my all!*

However, as glorious as chocolate may be, not even it beats a bowl of creamy, gooey macaroni and cheese with crumbled potato chips on top when you've got the just-stubbed-my-toe, the-toilet-leaks, the-kids-drive-me-crazy, think-I'll-curl-up-on-the-couch-and-watch-Oprah-since-it's-raining-out-and-I've-got-PMS-anyway blues. Cozy, comforting, stick-to-your-ribs (and thighs and belly) macaroni and cheese. Just saying the word *cheese* brings an instant smile to the lips. *Cheeeeese.*

Unfortunately, there's a catch. (There's *always* a catch.) It seems people who find their smiles in cheeeeese (and chocolate and cookies and Twinkies) also find that their clothes dryers mysteriously keep shrinking their pants. It's one of life's oddities that I've yet to figure out. Not only that, but as the pants shrink, the chins double. And the cheeks bulge—all of them. To make matters worse, as girth increases, the soul often grows lean, even unto death. Now isn't that a kick in the (too tight) pants?

So what do you do? You suck in your gut and wriggle into your control-top pantyhose. You shop for ankle-to-eyebrow girdles, drop all your friends who are thinner than you, and eat celery along with your morning Danish because you heard somewhere that it burns more calories than it contains. When all else fails, you go on a diet.

If you want my opinion, dieting is a major pain in the neck. Diets don't work. I can say that, having recovered nicely from them myself after dozens of tries. I won't bore you with all that I've attempted. You've probably done them too. The problem with diets is, one's focus is still on food—the not eating of it. When I'm dieting I wear a path into my carpet going back and forth to the kitchen as I chant something like, "Sweets are the destiny that shape our ends" and "Mmm, broccoli!" I call upon will power and any other power I can think of, but still end up "straightening out the crooked ends" of the cake in the refrigerator, and in the process eating more than if I had simply cut myself a slice.

My all-time favorite diet-related nonsense is where, after spending three or four hours opening and closing the refrigerator, lusting after the last piece of apple pie or the last two Kentucky Fried Chicken wings, smelling them, touching them, caressing them, when I can't bear it anymore I'll tell myself, "If I don't eat this, I'm just going to eat it, so I might as well eat it." (Note: A true "foodie" will understand the logic in that one.)

And then I'll eat it, and it will be heavenly…for all of a minute and a half. Then I'll hate myself for having given in. Again. Or, in a moment of defiance against whatever has been seducing me, I'll throw it into the trash, feeling victorious and proud…until I retrieve it later. (One of my tricks has been to pour liquid dish soap on leftover cake before I put it in the trash. Not even I would dig it out after that!)

It's a bulging battle, to be sure. Not only that, it eventually leads me to face that ultimate horror: the Doctor's Scale. Next to being caught naked by rescue workers or throwing up in public, what I fear most in life is a scientifically balanced, accurate-to-the-nth-degree doctor's scale. I much prefer the kind where you step on it with one foot and then place the toe of the other foot on the floor behind you and transfer your weight onto that foot while simultaneously pushing the wall in front of you with both hands. If you don't end up sprawled spread-eagle on the floor, you can easily weigh three or four pounds lighter. With a doctor's scale the most you can hope for is bad handwriting from the nurse who weighs you, making your 153 look like 128.

At my last annual checkup (which I always schedule in December near my birthday), the doctor took a look at my chart and said, "Well, we all put on a few extra pounds over the holidays." I thought to myself, *That's the nicest way anyone has ever told me I'm too fat.* In fact, I thought it was so sweet of him that I went home and baked an apple pie in his honor. I ate it in his honor too.

Held Hostage by a Hershey Bar

Can I be honest with you? I hate food. I hate it because I love it so much. Too much. I hate it because, as is characteristic with every idol, it has lied to me and I've fallen for the lies. It says to me, *I'm the sweetness your soul craves, the satisfaction your heart desires. I'm all you need. I'll make you happy. I'll be your friend.* It whispers in my ear, *What God has provided is not enough—* God *is not enough, but I am.*

But not even chocolate or macaroni and cheese can do and be all that. Still…I believe the lies and fall for food's seduction and keep on eating—and adding lies of my own. Here are a few of my favorites:

- A piece of Oreo cheesecake that you personally did not order but your dinner companion did technically has no calories. Thus, you can eat as much of his as you like.

- Calories in food eaten while standing bypass the stomach and flow directly through your legs and feet and onto the floor.

- Charitable foods such as bake-sale items purchased to help send needy kids to camp *must* be eaten. It's the virtuous thing to do.

- Certain foods, when eaten, don't count. They include food that doesn't taste good (but you eat anyway), food eaten in motion (such as in a car, plane, train, on foot, while in a rocking chair, etc.), any food smaller than one inch, and leftovers (the calories having seeped out overnight and transferred directly into the refrigerator light bulb).

- Food eaten after midnight doesn't count because you're half asleep and won't remember it in the morning. This correlates with the food-eaten-that-you-don't-remember-doesn't-count rule. If your brain can't remember it, then how can your hips remember?

- Breaking a cookie breaks the calories.

- When all else fails, drink diet soda, which acts as a purifying agent, washing away all unwanted calories.

Want to hear something pathetic? Sometimes, if I tell myself enough of these ridiculous lies, I start to believe them. But a lie, even if you believe it from the tip of your double chin down to your pudgy feet, is still a lie. Only the truth will set you free.

HOW MUCH IS THAT BROWNIE IN THE WINDOW?

Not only does every idol come with a lie, but it also extracts a price. *It makes you pay.* A few weeks ago, I was out driving and it was sweltering outside. I thought an icy coffee milkshake would hit the spot. Mmm. Unfortunately, I didn't have enough cash on me to buy one at Dunkin' Donuts, so I tried my hardest to put it out of my mind. However, that's like saying "Don't think about pink elephants." A coffee milkshake was *all* I could think of. So I suffered the agony of my deprivation until I could get home to make my own.

Like a junkie preparing her fix, I ransacked the cupboards until I found my blender, then carefully added the ingredients: vanilla ice cream, milk— and a coffee syrup that I made from three or four heaping spoons of instant coffee, some sugar, and a little water. I gave the blender a whirrr, then in sweet anticipation, s-l-o-w-l-y poured the whole thing into the biggest glass I could find, and drank the entire thing.

That's when it hit me. *I'd used regular coffee and not decaf,* which meant I had consumed the equivalent of six or eight cups of strong coffee in a matter of ten minutes—and I normally only drink one or two cups a day. For the next few hours, I paid the price, tearing around the house like a Tasmanian devil, chattering like a chipmunk, unable to sit still or even concentrate. I was still wide awake when the paperboy came at 4 A.M. That was one costly milkshake!

Sometimes, however, the price paid is much higher, especially when it involves guilt, shame, and fear. For example, I live in terror of coed potlucks. An all-female buffet I can handle since most women have food idiosyncrasies of their own and won't notice mine. But what I fear most is being in mixed company and having some man comment on my food, either the amount on my plate or my food choices. It's Harry Dawes in the fourth grade all over again. There I was in my maroon plaid dress purchased from the Fat Girls section at Sears (euphemistically named something like "Pretty Plus") when that creep Harry spotted me at the Sizzler with a plate piled high from the buffet. Although he probably didn't use a bullhorn and the restaurant loud speaker to get everyone's attention (as I had always thought), he did manage to announce, "You think you got enough there to eat?" Meaning, of course, *You could go without food for the next ten years and still have enough blubber to make soap.*

I'm forty-five years old. I haven't seen Harry Dawes since I was nine. But I still remember…and I'm still afraid, especially when I eat in mixed company (which I try to avoid at all costs).

Besides fear of buffets, food also evokes feelings of shame. Unless you've eaten a bologna-and-cheese sandwich while locked in the bathroom and then lied to your mother when she asked, "Who put bread in the toilet?" you don't know the power of food to bring shame.

I'm laughing as I write this, but the time and energy I spent concealing my eating from my mother wasn't funny. Neither was it funny the times I hid in the kitchen from my anorexic ten-year-old daughter, eating cake. Although she's fully recovered, when my daughter Alison was ten and eleven, she wouldn't eat. Couldn't eat. And as awful a time as that was for our family, it was compounded by an unseen struggle between her and me. Because I had always battled with my weight and with food, her thinness made me feel even worse about myself, so I would eat to try to feel better. To make matters nearly unbearable, because Alison learned from me that thin is good and fat is bad, her being thin meant she was superior and I was, therefore, inferior. She felt it and so did I, and I cowered in her presence.

Was it demonic? Well, chairs weren't flying around our house, but it smelled like smoke enough to realize Satan had a hold on the two of us, nonetheless. We were both held by food, either the eating of it or the not eating. What eventually happened to us I can only attribute to the merciful intervention of God. In a bizarre twist of circumstances, we both went on the same diet. Although she had intended to continue losing weight by eating what I ate, as I ate less and she ate more, we both began feeling better physically, then emotionally, and ultimately spiritually. I couldn't have orchestrated that if I had tried.

HE STILLS THE HUNGER OF THOSE HE CHERISHES

Throughout my life, whenever I've felt lonely or unloved, I've eaten. Whenever I've been bored, I've eaten. I eat for entertainment, for pleasure, for comfort and companionship. Mostly I eat when I'm alone, sometimes with people—but only with those I trust won't make me feel ashamed.

You can imagine how stunned I was at something I learned at a diet group and Bible study I joined (which I signed up for only because, after the pastor announced it, I thought if I didn't join, someone would tell me I should). I'm not going to tell you what I heard in the group about drinking lots of water and exercising and eating only until you start to feel full. You know that. *I* knew all that long before too. Everybody knows that! What everybody doesn't know—what I didn't know and maybe what you don't know—is this: *Food doesn't love me.*

I promise you I didn't know that. When I heard the group leader say that, I thought I'd spill the box of Junior Mints right out of my coat pocket! It took me awhile to chew on that statement until I could swallow it, but I eventually did. (Forgive me, I can't resist a bad metaphor.)

So if food doesn't love me, then what or who does? Well, my mother loves me; so does my dad and my husband and my daughters. One or two friends and my brothers and sister love me. They love me, and they can feed me (my mom makes a pork roast that will cause your eyeballs to pop out). But they can't still my hunger.

It doesn't take much to entertain me, and I especially enjoy finding obscure verses in the Bible that I secretly believe God placed there for my eyes only. One of my favorites is tucked into Psalm 17 where King David declared of the Lord in verse 14, "You still the hunger of those you cherish." I like that, don't you? It makes me wonder about King David. Like, did he have a problem passing up Sara Lee cheesecake or anything Hostess at the Winn Dixie like I do? Maybe he longed for a roast beef sub sandwich when he was out walking around Jerusalem. Or maybe, like me, he realized food (or whatever it was that he turned to for pleasure and comfort) didn't love him, but that God did. That when chocolate called out his name and told him lies, the Lord whispered in his ear, "I'm who you really crave. I'm the one you hunger and thirst after, and the only one who completely satisfies."

How does God satisfy? I don't know. I only know that he does. For when I'm starving, when my soul hungers to be fed, whenever I turn to him and not to whatever beckons from the pantry, when I open the Bible instead of the refrigerator and lift my heart and hands in prayer, he stills the hunger of the one he cherishes. That's *me*, dear friend. That's you, too.

Not only that, he's given us all food to enjoy: not just lettuce, but lasagna and garlic bread, fried catfish and hush puppies. The freedom to enjoy it comes when we remember that it's Jesus and not Snickers that truly satisfies.

So what do I do now when a triple-chocolate brownie calls out my name? Sometimes I eat it. Sometimes, though, I don't. Instead, I weigh the options and ask myself why I want it. *What will it do for me that Jesus can't?* The answer is always the same. *It can't do anything.* It can only make me feel worse. Knowing that doesn't make my choice easy, but it does make it easier. Besides, God always, always, always helps us when we make the choice for Christ. When I choose him, my hunger stills.

Think on These Things

1. We often classify certain foods as either "good" or "bad." Why do people give such distinctions?

2. One of the characteristics of an idol is that it is often a good thing to begin with, but then we elevate it to an ultimate thing. What do the following scriptures say about food and its proper place in our lives?

Isaiah 55:1-2

Luke 11:3

John 6:35

Matthew 4:4

Matthew 6:25

1 Corinthians 8:8

Ecclesiastes 9:7

Psalm 63:3-5

3. If food has been an idol in your life, write out a prayer to the Lord using the three *R's—repent, replace, rejoice.*

4. Read Psalm 17. Meditate on verse 14 (give yourself an extra bonus if you memorize it). Name some ways God "stills the hunger" of those he cherishes. What are your thoughts on being one whom God cherishes? Spend some time pondering this every day.

Bread of heaven, Bread of heaven. Feed me till I want no more.
—William Williams, "Guide Me, O Thou Great Jehovah"

Chapter 4

T.G.I.E.*
(*Thank God It's E-Mail)

There are a lot of activity addicts who'd love to stop running...
if they only knew how.—Chuck Swindoll

I happen to think e-mail is the greatest invention ever. Better than toasters with bagel-sized slots. Better than split-screen television or call waiting on your telephone. Even better than automated teller machines at the bank. For sheer speed and convenience (with the added bonus of zero face-to-face human contact, which only slows you down when you're in a hurry), you can't top it.

Just think, you can zip off a message to your sister in Detroit, your friend in Texas, and your mother in Fort Lauderdale within a matter of seconds, all without having to put on makeup or brush your teeth. Better still, you can do it *while* you put on your makeup and brush your teeth. You can even send the same exact message to all three and have each of them think you took the time to write a personal, individual letter.

I tell you, there's nothing like it, especially in today's busy world. It's a godsend. Now, if only there was a way to e-mail heaven…

TO: GODISLOVE@HEAVEN.UNIVERSE.ORG
SUBJECT: HELLO

Dear God,

Just a quick note to say hello and to tell you that I had planned to spend some time with you this week—honest, I did—but things just got away from me. I've been so busy lately! (But I guess you knew that already.) Just today I scraped the crud from between the stove and the counter, read the newspaper *and* listened to a book on tape while waiting to get my oil changed, and walked on my treadmill while watching a murder mystery on tape (the brother-in-law did it). Even before that I zipped over to the post office, dashed to the hardware store, made three phone calls on my cell phone while waiting in traffic, buzzed across town to get my eyebrows waxed, then raced back home in time for Bible study. I know I should've done my lesson, but you remember last week, don't you? Whew! That was a busy week, what with making party favors and table decorations for the women's retreat last weekend. I'm just glad I found that old devotion stuck in my desk drawer so I could use it on Saturday morning. Things were so hectic, I never would've gotten around to writing a new one. Besides, probably no one knew it was from two years ago. At least my mini-cheesecakes were a hit! That instant pudding idea, what a blessing.

You know, Lord, I really wish I had more time to make this e-mail longer, but I promised the pastor I'd disciple a new member of our church. I probably should prepare something, create a game plan at least, but I'm running late. I'll have to wing it. I told her I'd be at her house at 10:00 and it's already 9:45! Looks like I'm going to have to do my makeup in the car again. I just hope that this time I can balance my coffee cup better while applying my mascara.

I promise, one of these days when I get caught up on everything I'll spend a whole bunch of time with you. Maybe a combination retreat/vacation at the beach? I can work on my tan and think about you while I watch the ocean. Maybe by then I can even get around to listening to those sermon tapes I ordered last year.

Well, gotta skedaddle.

Love, your daughter

TO: MYCHILD@RUNNINGINCIRCLES.COM

SUBJECT: RE: HELLO

Dear Child,

Be still and know that I am God.

Love, your Father

TO: GODISLOVE@HEAVEN.UNIVERSE.ORG

SUBJECT: THE HURRIER I GO…

Dear God,

I know it's been a few days since you last e-mailed me, and usually I try to reply the same day, but I just can't seem to get it together. I'm jittery inside and feeling like that saying, "The hurrier I go, the behinder I get." I'm trying to get everything done, but nothing seems to be going right. I've got three loads of laundry and a washing machine that keeps going off balance and dancing across the laundry room floor; I just don't have time to stop and get it fixed. Can you maybe do something? I tried anointing it with cooking oil (does it matter if it's generic and not a major brand?) and saying a prayer. I'm not sure about the theology of that, but it worked once with my daughter's car!

Oh, Lord! Lately I've been feeling like I'm late for something. Like there's more to do than time in which to do it. I've got a stack of books to read and a list of new ones to buy. I need a haircut…but I honestly don't think I can squeeze in a trip to the hairdresser for at least two weeks. My mom's birthday card is sitting on the ironing board (which reminds me—I have a wrinkled shirt hanging in my closet). I need to call my aunt and pick up a paint roller at Wal-Mart. My husband asked me to return the drill bit he borrowed from our neighbor…and I have to call the termite man. Tomorrow's to-do list is already long, and I haven't even gotten through half of today's. I don't see how I'm going to get to this week's Bible study lesson. I feel so guilty; I'm thinking about skipping it altogether and getting the tires rotated on my car instead. That way I can go to the dry cleaner's *and* Wal-Mart, plus scribble a note to my mom while I wait.

What I'm trying to say is, it's not that I don't want to spend time with you. It's not that I don't love you or don't want to hear from you. I just want to be able to devote quality time to you. Right now I can't seem to find a moment's peace. Any advice?

On second thought, I'll work something out. I usually do. There's just so much to do…

Love, your daughter

TO: MYCHILD@RUNNINGINCIRCLES.COM
SUBJECT: MY ADVICE

Dear Child,

Be still and know that I am God. That's all you have to do.
Love, your Father

TO: GODISLOVE@HEAVEN.UNIVERSE.ORG
SUBJECT: YOUR LAST E-MAIL

Dear God,

Your last e-mail sounded a lot like your first one. (See—I'm paying attention.) And while I don't mean to be disrespectful, being still just isn't on my list. Baking sugar cookies and icing them to look like sunflowers for the spring bake sale (Did you see Martha Stewart's? *So cute!*) and freezing enchiladas for this week's microwave dinners, *that's* what's on my list. Isn't this what you've called me to do? Serve my family and my community?

I know my prayers to you lately are mostly on the run. (But remember when I prayed in line at the DMV last week? I would've gone insane if I didn't know you were there—it took forever.) You know how it is, Lord. It's a busy time we live in. Everything—everybody—goes so fast. Life goes so fast, and I'm doing my best to keep up. I'm trying hard, Lord. Really, I am. I'm trying to…to… Actually I'm not sure what I'm trying to do.

Can I be honest with you? The truth is, sometimes I feel like I'm stuck. Like there's a short in my circuitry. Like I can't slow down or stop even if I wanted to. I'm caught in a loop somewhere. Going around and around and around—and getting nowhere. Nowhere fast. Too fast!

Remember the time I got stuck on the Tilt-A-Whirl ride when I was in junior high? What fun! Twisting and twirling and spinning. There's nothing like that rush of whirling out of control. I remember screaming with laughter as the ride whipped us around. My friend and I were the only ones on the ride, and I remember wishing I could stay on forever.

But then it didn't stop. The guy at the controls winked at us and then didn't—wouldn't—push the stop button. I remember thinking he must have read my mind earlier and decided to grant me my wish. That's when it stopped being fun. The adrenaline rush turned to panic. My head throbbed from being jerked around, and I felt sick to my stomach. I kept praying the man would stop the ride so we could get off, but he just laughed. When he finally slowed down the ride and brought it to a halt, I was so relieved! What happened next, though, I'll never forget. We got off, bought another ticket, and went for another ride. Isn't that the most insane thing you've ever heard?

Lord, I don't know why I'm telling you all this, or even why I'm thinking about it after all these years. Right now I have phone calls to make—I signed up to help in the nursery and forgot that I'm already folding fliers for the missions' brunch (which reminds me, I promised to bake three extra quiches and need two dozen more eggs). Also, if you could bless my car, I'd appreciate it. I've got some errands to run, and the engine's a bit sluggish lately.

Oh, one more thing—the *e* key on my computer keyboard is sticking and slowing me down. Could you do something about that?

Love, your daughter

TO: MYCHILD@RUNNINGINCIRCLES.COM
SUBJECT: YOUR LIFE

Dear Child,

You are worried and upset about many things, but only one thing is needed. Remember this: In quietness and trust is your strength.

Love, your Father

TO: GODISLOVE@HEAVEN.UNIVERSE.ORG
SUBJECT: RE: YOUR LIFE

Dear God,

What you said about being "worried and upset about many things"— I've heard those words somewhere before. Oh, now I remember! Jesus said them to Martha when she was busy trying to fix dinner while her sister, Mary, sat in the living room with him. I've been meaning to ask you about that story. I've always thought Martha got a bum deal. Everyone talks about how Mary did the "better thing" by sitting with Jesus, but nothing would have gotten done if it wasn't for Martha! Who would've baked the lasagna or tossed the salad? Who would've crushed the ice for the lemon sorbet or picked out the perfect CD to set the mood for dinner? Who would've made the centerpiece? Who would've put out guest towels and scented soap in the bathroom? Lord, if you had taken all that away from Martha, what would she have had left? Who would she have been then, Lord?

Who would I be if you take away all that I do?

Love, your daughter

TO: MYCHILD@RUNNINGINCIRCLES.COM
SUBJECT: MY ANSWER

Dear Child,
> *Be still and know that I am God.*
> Love, your Father

TO: GODISLOVE@HEAVEN.UNIVERSE.ORG
SUBJECT: STILLNESS

Dear God,

I don't know if I can be still. It's not that easy! There's so much to do, and people depend on me to get things done. They call me "capable" and "dependable." I like that. It makes me feel important. Needed. Necessary. Like I matter and have significance and worth. Besides, I can't *not* do things! *I can't.* I need to be busy. It's what I do—it's who I am.

Sure, it gets tiring. Yes, sometimes my relationships suffer. I remember reading just last week that people who are always in a hurry have a diminished capacity to love. That love and hurry are fundamentally incompatible because love takes time—the one thing hurried people don't have.

I think a lot about the people in my life and the shallowness of my relationships with them. Sometimes when I'm with someone my mind's racing ahead to the next thing on my list. I plan on slowing down, Lord. Soon, too. This is just a busy season in my life. I'm sure my friends and family understand...don't they?

Love, your daughter

TO: MYCHILD@RUNNINGINCIRCLES.COM
SUBJECT: RE: STILLNESS

Dear Child,
> I'll say it again. *Be still and know that I am God.*
> Love, your Father

TO: GODISLOVE@HEAVEN.UNIVERSE.ORG
SUBJECT: RE: RE: STILLNESS

Dear God,

When you say "Be still," how still are we talking? Statue-still? Just slower than my usual pace? And for how long? An hour? A day? A year? And if I am still...what will happen to me? If I stop my whirling activity, if I cease doing-going-being for people, if I no longer fill my days with coming and going and helping and serving, what then? I've done this for so long, it's all I know how to do.

I'm afraid to do anything else. Afraid to do less. I'm afraid to be still— afraid to know that you are God.

There, I've said it. Now I'm afraid of what you might say to me. After all, you have been known to send people to strange, faraway places. Africa. China. Cincinnati. You told Jonah to go to Nineveh, and look where that landed him—inside a fish! I suppose the fish thing was his fault in the first place, since he ran away from you and all. But that only proves my point: When your people are still, you sometimes tell them to do ridiculous-sounding things. You told Noah to build a boat in the middle of a desert. You told Abraham to leave his home for a land unknown, and then you told his barren, octogenarian wife that she'd bear a child. You told Moses to stand up to Pharaoh the bully and Peter to walk on water. You've had your people march silently around the walls of a city and drink water from a rock. You told an unmarried virgin she would give birth to the Messiah.

Lord, it's a scary thing to be still and know that you are God!

Love, your daughter

TO: MYCHILD@RUNNINGINCIRCLES.COM
SUBJECT: A "SCARY" THING

Dear Child, *It is I.* Don't be afraid! Come to me. Hear me, that your soul may have life.

Love, your Father

TO: Godislove@heaven.universe.org
SUBJECT: Hurry sickness

Dear God,

I hear you, really I do. Just the other day I was reading something about "hurry sickness" (ironically as I was in a hurry at the dentist's office). At the time I didn't have the time to think it over, but now I recall the author saying, "The great danger is not that we will renounce our faith, but that we will be so distracted and rushed and preoccupied that we will settle for a mediocre version of it." Then he quoted Carl Jung: "Hurry is not *of* the devil: hurry *is* the devil."[1]

When I have more time I'd like to think that through. Right now there's a thirteen-hour housewares sale going on at the mall, and I only have two hours left to stock up on towels—and it will take me almost an hour to get there 'cause I have to swing by the bank first. I'll talk to you later, Lord.

Love, your daughter

TO: Godislove@heaven.universe.org
SUBJECT: Second thoughts

Dear God,

I'm back. I never made it to the housewares sale. I got out to my car and couldn't get out of the driveway—and it wasn't just because of the flat tire either. Even before I noticed it, I started thinking about something you said earlier. "Hear me, that your soul may live." So, right there in the driveway, I grabbed the Bible I keep in the backseat and looked up the passage in Isaiah, reading all about your invitation to come to you, to come to the waters and satisfy my thirst.

That's when I noticed my tire was flat...and that I was thirsty. You say come and buy wine and milk—without money and without cost. You ask, "Why spend money on what is not bread, and your labor on what does not satisfy?" Why hurry when what is important can't be rushed? Why spend your days in activity that doesn't feed your soul?

But it's hard, Lord. It's hard to say no. It's hard to stop. It's hard to be still. But, I'm not going to offer you excuses. I'm not even going to tell you I'll try harder. Work harder. Do more. That's the problem, isn't it? The trying and working and doing, when what you say is simply *be still.*

I confess, I don't know how to change, but I want to. I want to be free of this thing someone has labeled the "tyranny of the urgent." But…I'm scared. On the other hand, I'm tired. I don't know what to do except offer up my busyness and call it what it is: an idol in my life. I confess that I look to activity for significance instead of looking to Christ. I see now that while most of my activities are good, they are not what give me worth. Only you, Lord, can do that. Only you can bring life to my soul.

This turmoil I feel inside when I'm running here and dashing there is choking me. This "hurry sickness" is not only hurting my family, it's destroying my soul. I've just been too busy to see it.

You say, "Be still and know that I am God." I have a feeling you mean much more than sitting down for a daily quiet time where, as soon as I say amen, I get up and start running. No, I think you're talking about a constant quietness of soul, an inner calm that flows from an unshakable trust in your love.

I can't promise that I'll be still, Lord; I don't know that I can. But I do know that I need you.

Love, your daughter

TO: MYCHILD@RUNNINGINCIRCLES.COM
SUBJECT: YOU'RE CATCHING ON

Dear Child,

I know that you need me. That's why I've been telling you to be still. And don't worry; I'll help you. I've been doing this with your brothers and sisters for centuries!

By the way, in case you're thinking about fixing the tire on your car and trying to make that housewares sale...the spare tire's in the trunk, but you locked your car keys inside the car. So be still, my child, and know that I, indeed, am God.

Love, your Father

Think on These Things

1. If you could have three extra hours every day, how would you like to spend them? Now be honest: How would you really spend them?

2. Chuck Swindoll says, "Busyness rapes relationships. It substitutes shallow frenzy for deep friendship. It promises satisfying dreams but delivers hollow nightmares. It feeds the ego but starves the inner man. It fills a calendar but fractures a family." How true is that of your life? What "satisfying dreams" does busyness promise? How does it "feed the ego but starve the inner man"? Give specific examples.

3. Write out the following scriptures about stillness and quietness. (Bonus points if you rephrase them in your own words and personalize them by inserting your name.) When you're finished, note any inner changes—and rejoice!

Job 6:24

Isaiah 32:17

1 Peter 3:4

Psalm 107:29

Psalm 65:5-7

Psalm 23:2

Zephaniah 3:17

Psalm 62:1

Psalm 46:10

4. What are the benefits of a quiet spirit? What are some ways you can cultivate quietness in your life? Ask God to show you what you should weed out of your life, then ask him to (a) give you the desire to let go of it, and (b) give you the strength to do it. Keep in mind the words of Philippians 2:13, "God is working in you to make you *willing* and *able* to obey him" (CEV, emphasis mine).

Mid all the traffic of the way,
Turmoil without, within;
Make of my heart a quiet place,
And come and dwell therein.
—Author unknown

Chapter 5

She Who Dies with the Most Toys...Dies

The only reason a great many American families don't own an elephant is that they have never been offered an elephant for a dollar down and easy weekly payments.—Unknown

I couldn't pass them up. In fact, you wouldn't have expected me to. It would've been downright un-American of me. Dark forest-y green rayon pinstriped slacks, with teeny flecks of black in the fabric. They screamed out my name as I passed them by in the department store. They promised me they would fit perfectly—and they did. Then they sweet-talked me with those three magic words, "I'm on sale." Regularly $45.00, marked down to $38.99, then $14.98, then an additional 30 percent, *then another 70 percent.*

I ended up paying about $3.00 for a pair of pants that I neither needed nor wanted, but what a bargain! I'd hit pay dirt, whatever that means. I couldn't wait to get them home and find them a place of honor in my closet. All the way home I sang, "Three-dollar pants, I've got $3 pants. I'm so excited. And I just can't hide it. I'm about to lose control...'cause I got $3 pants. Oh, happy day! I got $3 pants today. Hey, hey, hey."

My car practically flew home, and I think I floated in through the front door with my precious $3 pants under my arm. I raced to my bedroom and opened up my closet, then carefully chose a spot in my dressy pants section, to the right of the two pairs of black slacks (one pair that I never wear), and to the left of the moss green pair (which I've only worn once). Then I sat on my bed to engage in one of my all-time favorite pastimes, namely, staring into my closet and admiring all my stuff. Of course, if anyone ever saw me doing that, I'd say I was praying or thinking about world hunger or pondering the five points of Calvinism. But between you and me, I just like looking at all my loot.

I love arranging all my clothes in my closet into categories and sorting them by color. I have my blazers over to the left, then my two long jumpers, then all my dressy shirts, dressy pants, jeans, casual shirts, and T-shirts. The colors go from dark to light, cool to warm. When I was younger, my favorite time of year was Back-to-School shopping. All summer long I'd lie on my bed and make lists of outfits for the upcoming school year. Again with the categories and the colors. The shopping was almost incidental. What I liked most then and now is the arranging of all my things...and knowing they're mine, all mine! Lots and lots and lots. Mine, mine, mine.

If you think that's pathetic, just wait until you hear this: I don't even particularly like wearing new clothes. I prefer my favorites, the worn jeans with the almost-holes in the knees, my baggy aqua sweater with the stretched-out neck. Many times I don't even take the price tags off things for weeks. I just like knowing that I have a certain item *just in case.*

Just in case I ever need two (identical) pairs of black slacks or five (also identical) white T-shirts, all I have to do is open my closet and—voilà! I have my dressy, churchy clothes, my crummy, clean-the-grout-in-the-shower-then-go-to-the-post-office clothes, and my medium, in-between clothes. *Just in case.* Just in case I ever get invited to a Victorian tea, I have my black floral jumper. Just in case I'm asked to an impromptu dinner party where the theme is "Salute to the Navy," I have my nautical blues and whites. Just in case I should take a midnight Caribbean cruise and the temperature on deck is 78 degrees and it looks like rain, I have a crinkle skirt and tank top that will keep me cool *and* not get damaged by rain. You never know…

IF YOU GIVE A PIG A PANCAKE

My new favorite book is *If You Give a Pig a Pancake* by Laura Joffe Numeroff. It starts off, "If you give a pig a pancake, she'll want some syrup to go with it." I like it because (a) I like pigs *and* pancakes, and (b) it shows a logical progression, cause and effect. When you do this, then this happens, which leads to this, which leads to that. It's a lot easier than trying to understand the laws of thermodynamics. I understand pigs wanting syrup on their pancakes. This leads me back to my closet, which leads me back to my $3 pants hanging in their place of honor directly in the center, which leads me to the fact that I had nothing to go with them.

Logic says, "Cut your losses; donate the pants to a charity thrift store," but Logic doesn't know about $3 pants. Because I had saved over $40, I was practically required by law to keep them. Not just keep them, but find something to go with them, something worthy of such a bargain.

After much thought, I decided what I needed more than anything was a sleek, collarless black jacket. The fact that I already owned three black jackets isn't the point. *They* all have collars, and one is short-sleeved. No, I definitely needed a collarless jacket to go with my $3 pants. After a week-long search, I found the jacket of my dreams…for $70 and not on sale. Sure, it cost more than I've ever paid for any one item of clothing in my life, but it fit perfectly and was exactly what I wanted. Except…I needed something to wear under it (or risk being arrested for indecent exposure or, worse, being laughed at).

As I sat down on my bed and stared into my closet, I realized two things: one, that I had nothing to go with my new jacket, and two, that what I needed more than anything to go with my black collarless jacket (which I needed to go with my $3 pants) was a white camisole made with Battenberg lace. *I needed it.* Unfortunately, the only one I could find was in a catalog for $19.95 plus shipping and handling. But since I needed it, what could I do? I had to buy it.

So the camisole came in the mail, which looked terrific underneath the black collarless jacket (which I needed for my $3 pants). As I put the outfit on and preened before my full-length mirror, admiring my finery (and congratulating myself on finding such a bargain as my $3 pants), panic struck: I needed new shoes to go with my new camisole with Battenberg lace, which looked great underneath the black collarless jacket (which I needed to go with my $3 pants). So, because I had already invested nearly $100 for the necessary accouterment to go with my $3 pants, I knew I couldn't let a pair of black pumps stand in my way.

One hundred fifty dollars later, I now have *the* most expensive pair of bargain $3 pants this side of the Mississippi. However, it's a great outfit, and if it wasn't so warm here in Florida, I could probably wear it. At least I know it's hanging in my closet just in case I'm invited to a soiree or a reception on a winter afternoon when the temperature is between 65 and 68 degrees.

See, if you give a pig a pancake, she'll want some syrup to go with it, and if you give me a bargain pair of $3 pants, I'll want everything else. Snort, snort.

NOT EVERYTHING, JUST *MORE*

It's not entirely true that I'll want everything. Take ceramic horses or Chinese art, for example. I don't want either of those. I have a Precious Moments ring box, and I don't want another. Neither do I want a wrought-iron birdcage to put plants in. I just don't want it. But I do want another coffee mug. I have a collection of them in my kitchen cupboard and only use three or four of them. But I think I'd like another one. Maybe two. Maybe another big cappuccino cup and saucer.

I also want more baskets in my house. One can never have too many baskets. I never use them, but I have them. They're stashed in corners, under tables, on top of my china hutch and tucked away here and there. I think I need another one. Several. Maybe a blue one. And a CD of thunderstorms. And one of crashing ocean waves. I want *more*. Not everything, just more. Not even more than you. I just want more, a little, teeny bit more than what I have now. More...and new.

That's part of the thrill—getting something new. Bringing it home and finding just the right place of honor and then looking at it. Looking and admiring and knowing that it's mine. *See those five white T-shirts in my closet? They're mine. Two are new. Got one on sale. They're all mine. All of them. M-i-n-e.*

Of course, I really don't think such thoughts. It's more of a subconscious thing. It's the pleasure I get from knowing that if I ever have the occasion to wear five white T-shirts at the same time, I can. If I ever need four black jackets and two pairs of black slacks all in one day, they're at my fingertips. If I ever have twenty-three people over and they all want coffee, I am secure in knowing I can accommodate them without any fights. And if there's ever a glut of peaches in my neighbor's yard and she hollers over the fence, "Hey! You got any baskets to put these peaches in?" I have the confidence to know that yes, I do have baskets. To actually let her use them is a different story altogether...

BIGGER, BETTER, NEW, AND IMPROVED

Or maybe it's the same story, like the story that Jesus told a crowd of people. He began, "Watch out! Be on your guard against all kinds of greed; a man's life does not consist in the abundance of his possessions" (Luke

12:15). He continued with a parable about a guy who produced a good crop. He had a lot of stuff and a bumper sticker on the back of his BMW that said, "He who dies with the most toys wins." He had *fifty* white T-shirts and a whole room full of baskets and cappuccino cups and saucers. His wife had thirty pairs of $3 pants (only she paid full price) and a separate room in their house just for her Beanie Babies collection.

But then the man discovered he had too much stuff—it was getting harder to squeeze between his Beemer and his wife's SUV in their garage, what with their new Harleys taking up so much room. So after soaking in his Jacuzzi for a while he decided he would tear down his existing garage and build a bigger one, plus an extra room off the den for his collection of Partridge Family memorabilia.

He called to his wife (who was on her StairMaster watching *The Price Is Right*), "Hey, Honey! Call the architect!" Then he took a sip from his bottle of imported spring water and thought to himself, *Yes, indeed. You have plenty of good things laid up for many years. Take life easy; eat, drink, and be merry.*

Unfortunately, the next day he was indicted for embezzlement and his wife ran off with the pool man. He spent the next twenty years in prison, and the IRS seized all his property (Luke 12:15-20, my paraphrase). Jesus told the people, "This is how it will be with anyone who stores up things for himself but is not rich toward God" (v. 21).

Right now I'm feeling a bit squirmy. I don't like that story. I like the stories Jesus told about finding lost sheep and angels rejoicing in heaven. This one lacks that certain warm, fuzzy quality. I like stories of abundant life, mercy, and grace. But this one gets a little too personal. It hits a nerve I'd rather not have anyone touch. It makes me feel naked. I want to be rich toward God, but I fear I've been too busy storing up things for myself so I can have more-more-more for me-me-me, thinking things will bring contentment. Not only don't they, but when I'm in hot pursuit of my next bargain, I also fail to appreciate what I already have.

PUTTING THINGS IN THEIR PLACE

God has given us all things to use and enjoy. Contrary to what some people believe, poverty is not a virtue and acquiring wealth and possessions is not sinful. But when I derive my sense of contentment from a packed closet, a cupboard full of Tupperware, or a linen shelf stacked with towels that no one is allowed to use, the things God has given me to use become idols.

Idols, by their nature, demand sacrifice. Bob Goudzwaard, in his book *Idols of Our Times,* writes, "We sacrifice for or to them other things of life, and thus become impoverished in those areas." He adds, "People are sacrificed for nations. Family life is sacrificed for business life; the best hours of a person's day are devoted to business, and the worn-out dog-ends of the day are left for family."

When it comes to my closet, I sacrifice my money for the sake of having *more*, my time in pursuit of that one more thing, my affections as I try to fill my heart with the pleasure derived from my abundance of things. But my soul stays lean. If my thoughts are centered on $3 pants to the exclusion of everything else—including God—I am guilty of idolatry. When I sit in church and think about shopping after the service, when I skip Bible study to get to the outlet center sale, when my prayer life is distracted by images of myself in that pink wool sweater I saw the other day at Lerner's, I am steeped in idolatry.

"Keep your lives free from the love of money," admonishes the writer of Hebrews, "and be content with what you have, because God has said, 'Never will I leave you; never will I forsake you'" (Hebrews 13:5). However, knowing that and doing that are two different things. *I like my stuff.* The question I need to ask myself is, To what extent will I go to hold on to those things? If I can't let go, if I fear their loss, then my possessions are more like my obsessions. I no longer own them; they own me.

The answer, however, is not to try harder not to want, because that won't work. Neither is the answer to vilify possessions and wealth. Rather the answer is first to admit things are too important in my life, to admit that I often turn to them first for significance, pleasure, comfort, security. Then I must decide what my heart really wants. If I find my significance or status in things, maybe what I really want is to know that I am important in someone's eyes. If it's comfort or pleasure, the thrill of acquiring something new, then maybe I'm using possessions ("shopping until I drop") to anesthetize boredom or an inner emptiness.

More than another new outfit, what I really need to possess is the knowledge that I have a Father who promised long ago that he would never leave or forsake me. That when the hurricane comes and blows the roof off the house and all my things are swept away, my Father is still there. When black jackets and $3 pants go out of style, my Father will still send his Spirit to comfort me and give me a reason to sing.

The late Corrie ten Boom once said, "I've learned that we must hold everything loosely, because when I grip (something) tightly, it hurts when the Father pries my fingers loose and takes it from me." I need to have that same attitude. Right now I don't think I do, but I'm making progress.

Last year we moved out of our three-bedroom house into a much smaller condo. As I took down my beloved possessions from the walls and shelves and realized the new place didn't have room for all of it, I packed them all up and gave them away. I haven't missed any of it. That's because nine years earlier when we moved from California to where we live now in Florida, we sold or gave away almost everything we owned, including our pine bed from when we were first married. How I loved that bed! But as I said good-bye to it I concluded that you can part with your things, but you can never part with your memories. Besides, stuff is just *stuff.* When you die, your heirs just have to go through everything and haul most of it to the dump or sell it at an estate sale. (Even $3 pants.)

There's a story of a little girl who loved a necklace someone had given her. One day her father set her on his lap and asked her, "Do you love your daddy?"

"Oh yes, Daddy!" she answered. "I love you lots!"

"Then give me your necklace."

This deeply troubled the little girl because she loved that necklace dearly. As the story goes, the father asked her several times to give him the necklace, but each time she couldn't. One day she did, and as she handed it over, her father pulled a strand of pearls out of his pocket and placed it around his daughter's neck. He had replaced her trinket with a dear and costly gift.

Sometimes—often—God does the same with us. We let go of a trinket, a raggy blankie, even a precious heirloom, and God replaces it with something finer. But sometimes he doesn't. Sometimes he simply says, "Never will I leave you; never will I forsake you."

> *Sometimes:*
> *The fig tree does not bud*
> *And there are no grapes on the vines,*
> *And the olive crop fails*
> *And the fields produce no food.*
>
> *Sometimes:*
> *There are no sheep in the pen*
> *And no cattle in the stalls.*
>
> *Yet:*
> *I will rejoice in the LORD,*
> *I will be joyful in God my Savior. (from Habakkuk 3:17-18)*

I've never had everything taken away from me all at once, and I hope I never will. I don't know how I'd react. I like my stuff! But...stuff wears out. It rusts and fades and shrinks in the dryer. It breaks and gets lost. It gets old, and we grow bored with it. On the other hand, God's mercies, his grace, his favor and delight are new every morning (Lamentations 3:23). They never wear out—and they're free!

She who dies with the most toys still dies. But she who sets her heart on possessing Christ lives.

Think on These Things

1. If you had five minutes to evacuate your house and rescue your most prized possessions, excluding people or pets, what would you save? Why?

2. Read Psalm 23. The first verse says, "The LORD is my shepherd, I shall not be in want." Another translation says, "I will never be in need" (CEV). What is the difference between want and need? What do you *want* that you may be telling yourself you *need?*

3. How does having the Lord as your shepherd help in your struggle to put possessions in their proper place?

4. In his book *Song of the Shepherd,* Mark A. Tabb says, "The Lord is my Shepherd, but the wolf is at the door." We may believe that the Lord is our shepherd, but we still question, *What if he doesn't come through? What if he doesn't provide?* How do the following scriptures quiet our doubts?

   Luke 12:32

   Psalm 37:25-28

   Matthew 6:25-34

   Matthew 7:9-12

   1 Timothy 6:17-19

In the fifth century, a man named Arenius determined to live a holy life.
So he abandoned the conforms of Egyptian society
to follow an austere lifestyle in the desert.
Yet whenever he visited the great city of Alexandria,
he spent time wandering through its bazaars.
Asked why, he explained that his heart rejoiced at the sight
of all the things he didn't need.
—Our Daily Bread, May 26, 1994

Chapter 6

Thighs of Jell-O, Abs of Flab

Gravity always wins.—Anonymous

I blame it all on my sister. As long as I've known her, she's always been a shy, quiet thing. Compliant. Easily molded by an ingenious older sister. I liked her mostly because I could tell her to do *anything* and she would, just because I said so.

"Peggy, we're going to eat dirt today," I'd tell her. Then she'd smile and nod her head and eat dirt. But then she had to go and grow up and get a mind of her own. A mind that decided exercise and keeping fit are a virtue. As for me, I've always believed that if God had wanted me to hop and jump and "pump, pump, pump-it-up" and holler "Woo!" (or sweat) he wouldn't have created overstuffed recliner chairs and remote controls. My idea of exercise is a brisk sit on a bench at the mall while I watch others in sneakers and carrying hand weights huff and puff past me. I say if an architect goes through all the trouble of placing an elevator in a building, then it's unkind of me not to use it. I say why run when you can walk? Why walk when you can ride? My motto has always been "No pain...*no pain.*"

And then my sister came to visit.

I hadn't seen her in years, not since I'd moved from California to Florida. Although she had stopped eating dirt even before I left, back then she was still a bossy big sister's dream of a personal plaything.

"Peggy, we're going to drop the kids off at Mom's, go get a haircut, then look at wallpaper." She'd smile, nod her head, and then do whatever I'd say.

"Peggy, we're going to the vacant lot across town." Again, she'd smile, nod her head, and ask, "Should I bring a spoon?" (A holdover from the earlier dirt-eating days.)

I wasn't prepared for the sister who came bounding and bouncing down the airport terminal. I took one look at her and knew my days of pushing my baby sister around had come to a halt. A muscular, aerobic, Jazzercised halt. She could definitely whup me.

She flexed her arms and gave me a hug that could crack a coconut. Then she did some sort of bouncy, kicky thing with her feet, tossed her head from side to side, and clapped her hands. "Woo!" she cried. I got winded just watching her.

To my sister's credit, she kept her Jazzerstuff to herself all the way back to my house from the airport, even though I knew she was dying to spread her gospel of perfect pecs—especially after she had a chance to see me lumbering around the airport looking for a baggage cart to hitch a ride on.

She did, however, convince me to go for a stroll with her once we got home. I agreed only because I had to go to the end of the driveway anyway to check the mail. Did I say we went for a stroll? I may have strolled, but Peggy trotted. Or was it sashayed? Maybe she clipped. At any rate, she clearly passed me by, kicking dust all over me in her wake.

Although I'm only three years older, next to my sister's trim, toned, 22 percent body-fat body, I felt not unlike the mounds of dough my great-uncle Benny used to heave onto the bread tables at our grandmother's bakery. I remember watching the dough wiggle and jiggle until it finally came to a blobby halt. When Uncle Benny wasn't looking, I'd poke my finger in the dough to make it jiggle again. *That's* what I felt like.

Actually, even before my sister came to visit I had entertained a fleeting thought or two of getting into shape. It's not that I wasn't in shape, it's just that my shape was round…and soft…and doughy. I made a perfect pear, I thought. Good center of gravity, aerodynamically sound. Not easy to tip over. Except…I'd been feeling a bit…I believe the technical term is *yucky*. Blah. Blech. Like an unbaked loaf of Uncle Benny's rye bread before it went into the oven. I could shake, rattle, and roll, all without moving a muscle.

By the time Peggy and I came back from the grueling trek to the mail-box—me all sweaty and clutching my sides, Peggy all smiles and without any extra padding on her sides to hold even if she needed to—I had made a decision. But since my original idea is a capital offense, I decided against stuffing my sister in a mailing tube and sending her back to California and decided instead to beat her at her own game. Fight fat with whatever one fights it with.

So you could say Peggy's visit was a good thing. Martha Stewart might say that. But I'm not going to. I'm just going to blame what followed all on my dear sister.

DISCOVERING THE INNER "WOO!"

I waited until Peggy returned to California, then I got to work. First I took a nap, then a bath. Then I got my hair cut and bought a rug for the bath-room. Yes, I know not one of those activities moved me closer to my goal of Getting into Shape, but when your most strenuous form of exercise has been limited to running your mouth and jumping to conclusions, you have to ease into these things. So the next day I did a leg lift and considered touching my toes. The day after that I rested. But the following day I dis-covered the "Woo!"

Peggy had explained *wooing* to me. She said you work and sweat and pump, pump, pump-it-up until you reach a point where you just have to holler, and what you usually holler is "Woo!" Of course, she meant holler because exercise supposedly feels good. I hollered because I tripped on my unlaced sneaker and ran into the corner of the coffee table and bruised my thigh. *Woo! That hurt!* It took a week and a half of complete recliner-chair therapy to get me up and rolling again.

Fortunately (or unfortunately, depending on your point of view) I hadn't damaged anything permanently during my coffee-table mishap. Also fortunately (or un) Peggy had overnight expressed me a pair of bike shorts and a Jazzercise T-shirt to help get me motivated. They didn't. At least not from the package. However, the struggle to pull the shorts up and the subsequent view in my full-length mirror worked motivational magic once I discovered I had more rolls around my middle than Uncle Benny ever had in the roll bin at the bakery. Reality may be cruel, but one needs a bite from it every so often. That's where my search for the inner *Woo!* began. Or at least my quest for a perfect body.

After viewing myself in exercise shorts (picture a tube of refrigerator biscuits that just exploded), I discarded the whole I-have-to-beat-my-sister contest. No, I had a bigger goal in mind, namely, my hips. My thunderous thighs. My upper arms that hadn't seen daylight ever since they grew wings because I've kept them covered. My dimpled cheeks and gluteus maximus.

Strangely optimistic, I picked up a magazine Peggy had left behind. "Flatten Your Belly in Just Two Weeks!" it promised on the cover. Another article vowed I could melt 800 calories a day doing some sort of a kicking, punching thing called Tae Bo. Yet another article guaranteed "perfect pecs" and "absolute abs," and still another pledged everything from glowing skin and shinier hair to whiter teeth and a cure for acne through aerobic house-cleaning. ("Bend and stretch and swipe that cobweb!" and "Don't cry over spilled milk—do jumping jacks instead!") Then there were the usual sit-ups, pull-ups and the other "ups" that help defy the law of gravity for a middle-aged mother of two. Despite my previous four-decade-long goal to see how long I could go without breaking a sweat, I jumped into my plan to Get in Shape with both thighs jiggling.

I won't go into the various exercises I started doing because I'm sure you've seen them on TV. Just know that I did them all. I also invented the laundry lunge and cardio carpooling. (That's when you stick your left arm out your car window and your right arm in your passenger's face and make tight arm circles while stopped in traffic. It embarrasses your passenger and angers other drivers, but it does wonders for that pesky excess underarm overhang.) I set my alarm so I could walk on my treadmill before sunrise, raced through my day to maintain my optimum pulse rate, wore ankle weights everywhere but the shower, and carried around a set of calipers to measure my body fat every few hours.

Although I wasn't aware of it, according to my friends and family, it seems I had crossed an invisible line. Some say I had snapped. One called it "going aerobically postal." Bonkers. But I'd set my sights on the goal. I was running my race, out to win the prize—pressing on toward the mark of the high calling (of Getting into Shape). After all, isn't that what the Bible says?

No longer content with a potatolike existence on my couch, I'd found that missing "something" within. That drive to achieve. My *raison d'être*. Not to mention looking less lumpy in my bike shorts. *Woo!*

For those who know me, I tend toward the obsessive-compulsive side of sanity, and my newfound passion for Getting into Shape proved no exception. Only I couldn't see it. Once I plunge (or in this case, lunge and leg-lift) myself into something, I tend to lose all sense of anything else. It's as if my entire being only knows one setting (turbo) and one direction (straight ahead). Whatever my goal is, from being the World's Laziest Slug to Fitness Queen of the Universe, I throw myself into it wholeheartedly.

I also tend to lose all sense of God along the way.

Plain and simple, here's how it goes: I decide to make a change in my life. Do something good, set a goal. So far, not a problem. I plan and plot and take the first few steps. I discover I like the feeling of success, or at least of progress, as I head in the right direction. Still, not a problem.

I pray; I give thanks to God. I seek him at every turn. If it's exercise, I acknowledge that he's the one who made me. If I'm out of shape, I ask his forgiveness for not taking care of myself and ask for his help. My desire is to honor him with my body, and I begin exercising as an act of stewardship. All is well with my soul.

But then something shifts. I start to lose weight—I fit into the pair of jeans I've had stashed way in the back of my closet. I begin to look at myself in the mirror instead of covering my eyes. I look closer. *Closer*. I examine every inch and make mental notes: *If I lost two more inches in my hips and maybe one in my waist...if my stomach was flatter...I really hate the way my calves look...I wonder how I could tighten the upper part of my thighs...*

At my next workout I do just one more set of leg squats. One more set of arm curls. Twenty more minutes on the treadmill. I begin planning my whole day around my workout. I worry if I think I won't be able to get to it and feel guilty if I miss. It takes up too much of my thinking time and much of my conversation. What started out as a good thing, a healthy thing, grips me so tightly I can barely breathe—and I don't even know it. All I know is, I'm not free.

WHO RAISED THE BAR?

The idol in my life is not exercise, it's *me*. It's always me in one form or another. In this case it's me trying to gain control or master an area of my life. It could be anything: maintaining a spotless kitchen floor, growing the most enviable garden, baking a better peach cobbler than my mother-in-law's. Trying to outdo Kenny G on the saxophone or making *this* Christmas the best one ever. It's achieving for the sake of achieving, with no tangible or measurable end in sight. Someone (me?) keeps raising the bar, moving the goal. I can't reach it!

When I'm held by achieving, I never quite make it because my ultimate goal (a better/happier/easier/more satisfying life) is only an illusion, like a desert mirage. Just when I think it's within my grasp, it's gone and I'm left frustrated and angry.

I don't know about you, but I hate being frustrated. It's so...*frustrating*. Have you ever had someone break a promise to you? You had your hopes up, your heart set on going to the Bahamas or Walt Disney World or Wal-Mart, or someone promised to love you forever then never followed through and it left you wondering whatever happened to the happily-ever-after you were sure you'd find. Friend, that's what idols do—and that's one of the reasons God says we're not to place any idols before him. He knows they only disappoint us (at best) and destroy us (ultimately) as we chase after them and hold on tight. Fortunately, he loves his children too much to stand idly by while we seek satisfaction in other things, although he often allows us to try and stops us when we've gone far enough. Sometimes he sends storms and giant fish, as he did with Jonah. Sometimes, as he did with me, he sends a pinched sciatic nerve.

MUSINGS FROM THE FLOOR

Funny thing about idols and clinging to them. We try our hardest not to let go, even when we're on the floor in pain. I'm not sure what I did, but whatever it was, I don't want to ever do it again! I wish I could describe the pain that shot down my leg. It was so intense that I wanted to take a knife and stab it. The only relief I could find was on my stomach on the floor with my injured left leg bent to the side. For three weeks I lay on the floor, unable to do anything except think.

The first few days I thought about the utter unfairness of my situation and how cruel life is and how God had abandoned me. (I've always been a tad on the melodramatic side.) Then I calculated how I could get back to my workouts once God saw the error of his ways by putting me on the sidelines. I begged for healing, pleaded for mercy. I watched my Denise Austin exercise tapes, hoping her working out could be commuted to me through osmosis.

Then God spoke. Or maybe the wind blew. Either way, I heard the words of Solomon, the wisest man who ever lived: "Yet when I surveyed all that my hands had done and what I had toiled to achieve, everything was meaningless, a chasing after the wind" (Ecclesiastes 2:11).

"So what are you saying, Lord? That I shouldn't attempt anything because it's all meaningless?"

Child, goals and dreams and working toward them are good. Calculating how many extra calories you'll burn if you increase your treadmill speed instead of paying attention during your pastor's sermon is not good.

"Oh, you know about that?"

Did you think I wouldn't? I know all about you, Child. That's why you're on the floor. I know you need to be here. Trust me, you'll thank me for this someday.

One gets a whole new perspective on life while on the floor. The only direction to look is up. So since I couldn't do anything else, I looked up—and discovered a God who knew me. A God who knew me and loved me enough to lay me out flat on my face. It was the only way he could get my attention.

What if I reached the goal—Got into Shape—what then? What if I did finally get my kitchen floor spotless or actually had the best Christmas ever? What would it get me? Would it get me more love or respect? Complete soul-satisfaction? Inner peace and a final end to all my striving?

In two words: no brainer. Of course my trying hard won't get me any of that! So why do I keep trying? What is it that I really want?

Let's face it, even if I did finally achieve the perfect body, a table centerpiece even Martha Stewart would envy, or a floor clean enough to lick, I still wouldn't be content. I'd raise the bar, set my standard even higher, or in the case of the clean floor, work nonstop to maintain it—and probably alienate my family in the process as I chased after them with a mop.

There's just something in me that needs to know that I accomplished something so people will say about me, "Isn't she something special?" So I will say that about myself. So God will say that about me. As with any idol, making a personal goal my god devalues Christ's death by holding up my achievements in its place. What I'm saying is, "Jesus is not enough—I need perfect abs too."

On the other hand, what if I had another goal? What if my goal was to know God? Jesus prayed that I would. Recorded in the gospel of John, on behalf of you and me he prayed, "This is eternal life: that they may know you, the only true God, and Jesus Christ, whom you have sent" (John 17:3).

Is it possible to know God? The only true, most holy God? It has to be, otherwise Jesus wouldn't have prayed it.

As his child, the goal most worth pursuing in life is knowing my Father. Knowing him through his Word, his wonders of creation, the works of his hands, the revelation of his Spirit within me. He says to his people, "Know therefore that the LORD your God is God" (Deuteronomy 7:9). "Be still, and know that I am God" (Psalm 46:10). How can I do this? He answers, "I will give them a heart to know me, that I am the LORD" (Jeremiah 24:7). Knowing God is something I can achieve.

Not only that—I've saved the best part for last—even greater than knowing God is being known by him. Just think: the Maker of the ocean waves that crash on the rocks of the Pacific Northwest coast, the Designer of peacocks and panda bears (and Brad Pitt!) knows me intimately and personally, and he reveals himself so I may in turn know him. Know his goodness, kindness, and mercy. Know that he is on my side, that he fights on my behalf, that he has my name written on the palm of his hand. Know that, despite my weaknesses and flaws and my propensity to go overboard trying to find something that can only be found in him, he loves me. He knows me, and he loves me anyway.

Now that's something to make you holler *Woo!*

Think on These Things

1. What area of your life would you like to master or get under control once and for all? If this happened, how would your life be different? How realistic is this expectation?

2. In his book *Knowing God*, J. I. Packer says, "Once you become aware that the main business you are here for is to know God, most of life's problems fall into place of their own accord." What does it mean to "know" God? What means has God given us to help us know him?

3. Concerning knowing God, what is implied in the following passages?

    Romans 1:18-20

    John 17:26

    Psalm 9:10

    Jeremiah 24:7

    Jeremiah 9:23-24

    Philippians 3:7-10

4. What is the evidence in a Christian's life of knowing God? See the following verses:

2 Corinthians 12:9

Galatians 4:6

Galatians 5:1

Ephesians 3:16

Philippians 4:7

Philippians 4:13

Philippians 4:19

Hebrews 12:10-11

For what higher, more exalted, and more compelling goal can there be than to know God?
—J. I. Packer, *Knowing God*

Chapter 7

The Disease to Please

"Does everybody in the world have to like you?"
"Yes, yes! Everybody in the world has to like me! I must be liked!"
—conversation between Jerry Seinfeld and George Costanza, *Seinfeld*

I grew up Nice. Born into a Nice family to Nice parents who raised four Nice children. We are certified, bona fide, capital *N* Nice. Terminally Nice. We even had Nice neighbors. One time the ladies who lived next door to us caught my brothers lighting matches on the side of the house (a youthful lapse of their usual Niceness), and the women felt so awful for having to rat on the boys that they brought over an electric popcorn popper as a gift. We thought it was So Nice of them that we—while I don't know this as a fact, but knowing how Nice we are—reciprocated with a gift of our own. Green Jell-O with applesauce, as I recall. We probably insisted they keep the plate too. After all, that is the Nice thing to do.

Want to know how Nice I am? I apologize to bugs before I kill them. When I'm in a merge-traffic situation and I don't know who to be Nice to first, the driver who wants me to let him in or the one behind me who doesn't want me to, I've been known to pull over and let the whole line of cars go by so I can be Nice to everyone.

I'm so Nice that I always return a store clerk's "Have a nice day!" with a big smile and a "You, too!" Even if she was rude and I don't want her to have a nice day. (And then I feel guilty for not wanting her to have one.)

I'm so Nice that I feel guilty if I'm sick around healthy people, but feel even guiltier if I'm healthy around sick people (because they're sick and I'm not). How inconsiderate of me!

I'm so Nice that when someone cuts me off in traffic, I smile and wave and try to look as winsome as I can so they won't hate me for their ignorance.

I'm so Nice that if someone calls at 3 A.M. and wakes me up asking if I'm Ed's Towing, I immediately apologize for not being Ed, then I may even offer to get the phone book to look up Ed's number.

I can't say no, even to things I really, really, *really* don't want to do because I feel guilty. First I feel guilty for not wanting to do the thing, then I feel guilty because if I say no, the person will have to go through all the trouble and aggravation of calling someone else.

I never hog parking places, never walk through a door ahead of anybody. I always compliment the chef and bring a hostess gift. I send thank-you notes and draw happy faces on my checks when I pay my bills. I'm a pleasure to work with. I play well with others and always share my toys. I'm a model employee. I don't yell, hit, kick, scratch, or bite. Usually. I'm mostly careful to keep all negative feelings bottled up Nicely until they do a Mount Vesuvius and explode all over, killing innocent people in their wake. But since that's not very Nice, I try not to do that too often.

The problem with Niceness is, it isn't always Nice. As an idol, it's narcissistic and dishonest. I am Nice to preserve my image so I can gain approval—even from people I don't like. Niceness is manipulative, a means of controlling people. *Because I'm so Nice, you can't help but love and approve of me. If you don't, well, there's something wrong with you.*

A few years ago I inadvertently offended a friend. The details aren't important except to say I honestly didn't mean to offend her. (I'm too Nice for that.) But I did, and she was angry and let me know it. She had every right to. As a Nice Person, I allowed her to yell at me. In fact, I helped her.

I agreed with everything she said and added a few self-accusations of my own. I apologized many times over. I was sincerely sorry she was angry at me. Sincerely sorry to be the target of someone's anger. Profoundly sorry that she no longer thought of me as one of the Nicest people you would ever want to meet.

I called her; I wrote her letters. But I would not open myself up for any type of emotional intimacy. Instead, I used my Niceness as a defense and to keep her at arm's length. *As long as I'm the Nice one, I'm still okay. As long as I'm Nice first, I've done my part. You're the one responsible now.*

How Can You *Not* Like Me?

My friend Sandra, a recovering Nice Person, got her teeth kicked in (figuratively) when someone told her, "You know, Sandra, not everyone's going to like you." She told me her face burned with embarrassment as she thought, *How can that be? Isn't that the whole idea?*

I tossed this idea around to a few of my other Nice friends. I e-mailed one friend and asked her, "What if you found out someone didn't like you? What would you do?" Immediately she returned a frantic message. "Why? Do you know somebody who doesn't like me?" Then she added, "If I thought someone didn't like me, I would assume it's all my fault. I'd mentally go over every single thing we ever did together and every conversation we've ever had to figure out what I did wrong. Then I'd probably die."

I know all about the probably dying part. Long ago I contracted the "disease to please" (as someone on *Oprah* once called it), and it has taken its toll. There are three women in my community (that I know of) who don't like me, and it's *killing* me. One just started not liking me, and one hasn't liked me for a few years. The other one began her intense dislike of me when our daughters were in fifth-grade Safety Patrol together.

We had both been chaperones on the summer trip to Washington, D.C., and on the second to the last day there, I Mount Vesuvius-ed all over her. She had yelled at me and, uncharacteristic as it is for such a Nice

Person like myself, I yelled back. In front of God and the Safety Patrollers and all the other chaperones. Of course, I was the wounded party, being the Nice One, and everyone took my side, which made this other woman not like me even more.

It made for an excruciatingly long bus trip home to Florida, what with me dying and all. As soon as we got back I immediately wrote her a long, rambling letter, confessing my grievous sins and begging her forgiveness. I didn't hear back from her, which was a relief since I didn't really want any human contact with her ever again, only an acknowledgment that I'm not the most despicable creature on the planet, but am, in fact, still Awfully Nice.

After a few weeks I still hadn't heard from this woman, so I sent her another note. Something inside compelled me to make her like me. I forced my daughter to give her daughter candy on the school bus, and I made sure I always waved and smiled if I passed her on the road. However, when she showed no response other than to ignore my pathetic attempts to make her think I'm still Nice, I began hiding from her. We live in a small town and our daughters go to the same school, so this is no small feat. I had to determine what market she shopped at and when (so I could do my grocery shopping elsewhere), which route she took to work, where she might happen to pop up on a Saturday afternoon, and whether or not she would attend the Friday night high school football game.

It worked for several years, and I became rather proficient at pretending to be fascinated with the programs handed out at the door at Back-to-School Night as she passed by me in the auditorium. I dreaded the day our daughters would have classes together and we would have to meet face to face during the Meet-the-Teacher part.

Then the inevitable happened. I had taken a holiday job wrapping Christmas gifts at the only department store in our town. I was pretty sure if she happened to be shopping while I was there and wanted her gifts wrapped that she would come back another time when I wasn't there. Still, there was that chance, and I kept a watchful eye out for her at all times.

Then the store had a sidewalk sale, and all employees had to take turns outside guarding the merchandise. On the day it was my turn, I saw her out of the corner of my eye and immediately froze. At that moment I knew what a deer feels like when it senses a hunter has it in his rifle sight. That's when I did what I do best—I panicked and jumped into a rack of clothes to hide.

Surrounded by beaded sweaters marked down by 40 percent, with men's polo shirts on top of my head, I watched and waited. *The woman would not go away!* I had to do something. Anything. So knowing this woman hated me, yet praying fervently that she didn't even remember me, I climbed out of the clothes rack as nonchalantly as I could and eked out a "Hello there."

Of course she recognized me. (You don't tend to forget people who explode all over you and embarrass you in front of a hundred people.) I offered her yet another apology, which she graciously accepted. We did the It-was-all-my-fault/No-it-was-all-*my*-fault routine. Then she turned and walked away, and I returned to my sidewalk sale duties.

All's well that ends well, right? In TV sitcoms and romance novels maybe, but not necessarily in real life. A few months ago I found out that this woman still hates me—and tells everyone what kind of person I am. And it doesn't rhyme with *rice*.

I can't understand it. I'm So Nice—how can she not like me?

Remember I told you about my friend Sandra whose friend "kicked her in the teeth"? Well, I got a teeth-kicking myself—by my own dear husband, no less. The other day when I was telling him about this chapter I'm writing on Niceness, he innocently asked, "Who is it about?"

I stood in the kitchen, stunned. *He doesn't know it's about me?*

So I asked him, "You don't think I'm Nice?" This honestly wasn't a trick question like my occasional Do-you-think-I'm-fat? that has no right answer. I couldn't comprehend that he didn't know what a Nice Person I am. We've only been married twenty-five years!

"Well, it's not that I think you're un-Nice," he replied. "You're Very Nice to other people. You just act 'regular' to me."

"Is that a good thing?" I asked him.

"Am I complaining?" he answered.

Regular, huh? I'm still thinking that one over.

THE ANTIDOTE!

The truth is, being Nice is awfully tiring. I'd much rather be "regular." It helps to remember what author Steve Brown often reminds his readers and listeners: "Jesus didn't die to make us nice. Jesus died to make us his." Even before that, J. I. Packer said we don't have to be nice because we have been adopted. In his classic book *Knowing God,* he calls adoption the basis for our life, "the highest privilege that the gospel offers—higher even than justification."

He adds, "Adoption is a *family* idea, conceived in terms of *love*, and viewing God as *father.* In adoption, God takes us into his family and fellowship—he establishes us as his children and heirs. Closeness, affection and generosity are at the heart of the relationship. To be right with God the Judge is a great thing, but to be loved and cared for by God the Father is a greater."

In his own way, my husband had said something similar. On a human level, because I feel secure in his affection and commitment to me—his *approval,* which is what Niceness really seeks—I don't have a neurotic need to overly please him. On the other hand, with those whose approval I'm not sure of, I knock myself out trying to earn their favor, which only sets me up for disappointment.

That's another characteristic of an idol. It disappoints and disillusions. Niceness lies and says, "Act a certain way, be all things to all people, let them walk all over you—be sure to smile, smile, SMILE—and everyone will love you. You'll be A-OK." But you know as well as I do that that's just not true. There's always a fifth-grade Safety Patrol mom out there who drives you to hide in clothes racks and make you feel *not* A-OK.

God knows this about idols. That's why the Bible uses words like *worthless* to describe them and then shows us something better than Niceness—the security of adoption and the specialness of being chosen as God's own child. "He predestined us to adoption as sons through Jesus Christ to Himself," the apostle Paul wrote to the church in Ephesus, "according to the kind intention of His will, to the praise of the glory of His grace, which He freely bestowed on us in the Beloved" (Ephesians 1:5-6, NASB). No longer a slave, but a son (Galatians 4:7) with all honor, rights, and privileges of sonship. Once and for always, forever and ever, by grace. He didn't die to make us nice; he died to make us his.

The Fruit of the Spirit Is...*Not* Niceness After All

So if Jesus didn't die to make me Nice, how then am I supposed to live? Can I go around tripping old ladies in the grocery store? Obviously I can't. But then...what? It helps if I think of it this way: Niceness is the counterfeit. It's phony, fake, plastic, and pretentious. Niceness is other-centered actions with self-centered motives.

Kindness, on the other hand, is a fruit of the Spirit, a natural by-product of a life that draws its nourishment from God and finds its outlet in acts of mercy. Because God has chosen me as his own and adopted me by his grace, I am secure. Because I'm secure, I'm not compelled to be Nice. Instead, I'm free to be kind. I'm free to say no to things I don't want to do. I'm free to be disliked by people and free to believe that it's okay and that it doesn't mean there's anything wrong with me. I can be "regular" and still be accepted.

That, my friend, is nice to know.

Think on These Things

1. In what ways can Niceness be thought of as a Christian virtue? How is it deceptive?

2. What does it mean to be adopted? What are some of the rights and privileges of being a son (or daughter) of God? Use these scriptures to help you:

   John 1:12-13

   Galatians 4:4-7

   1 John 3:1

   Ephesians 1:5-6

   Matthew 6:25-32

   Matthew 7:11

3. How does being secure in your adoption free you from the need to be Nice? What is the difference between being *nice* and being *kind?*

4. Read Colossians 3:12-17. Take note of the tone of this passage and the words Paul used in his instruction to the Colossians. In thinking about the discussion of the "disease to please," which words, thoughts, or phrases strike your attention? Why? How can this passage help a person find freedom from this particular idol?

―――――――――

God will go out of his way to make his children feel his love for them
and know their privilege and security as members of his family.
Adopted children need assurance that they belong,
and a perfect parent will not withhold it.
—J. I. Packer, *Knowing God*

Chapter 8

Give Me a Brake!

Good Morning. This is God. I will be handling all of your problems today.
I will not need your help. So relax and have a good day.
—read on a refrigerator magnet

You would think that after knowing me all these years my daughter wouldn't be surprised, but she was—along with annoyed, humiliated, embarrassed, and all the other adjectives and epithets teenage daughters fling at their mothers. Especially mothers who suggest placing a magnetic sign on the side of the family car that says "Student Driver—Stay Away from My Kid!"

At the time I thought it sounded like a good idea. Just that added measure of safety, like a maniac-driver repellant acting as an invisible shield protecting her as she learns to drive. I know when I see a Student Driver sign on a car, I always keep my distance. I assume other drivers do the same. So why not carry the idea over to the family car? Why not advertise to the world that my precious baby girl is out on the perilous and treacherous highway and that all other drivers had just better stay away?

At the time I suggested it, it made complete sense to me. I still like the idea. My daughter, however, has other thoughts on the subject, to put it mildly. She has the wild notion that I don't even want her to drive, but that's not true. I want her to drive, I just don't want her to crash. So I have rules…

Before every driving lesson we first check the most current weather report. Anything over a 30 percent chance of rain, I drive. Laura says it's because I think at the first drop of rain she'll throw the car in reverse, flip the hood up, and recline the seat trying to find the windshield wipers. She's got me on that one. I don't mean to think that, but I do. *After all, it could happen.*

Another rule: No driving on holidays. Or the day before or the day after a holiday. If it's a major holiday with lots of celebrating, say for a whole month, then no driving for that entire month. No driving at night. No driving at noon. No driving at twilight or rush hour.

I don't allow driving if the sun's too bright, since you can't always trust sunglasses to cut the glare no matter what the commercial says. There's definitely no driving without a full eight hours' sleep the night before. And there's no driving if I didn't get a full eight hours' sleep as well. (Of course, I can drive under those circumstances since everyone knows mothers are trained to operate heavy machinery in a sleep-deprivation mode.)

It's not as if I never let her behind the wheel. I let her start up the car in the mornings and turn on the radio. And when the circumstances are to my satisfaction (like when everyone's off the road), I let her practice. That is, if she passes the pop quiz:

ME: "Okay, what would you do if a car cut in front of you?"

HER: "I'd put on my brake."

ME: "What if you hit a puddle?"

HER: "I'd pump my brake slowly."

ME: "What would you do if you hit a squirrel?"

HER: "I'd gag but keep going."

ME: "Okay, what would you do if a tomato truck and a horse trailer collide up ahead of you and at the same time your oil light goes on and the radio announces a thunderstorm warning and you have a gallon of ice cream melting in the backseat and a bee flies in your window?" *Again, it could happen.*

To my credit, I do let Laura drive to the market. Sometimes. Only because it's 2.2 miles with no left turns. And one time I let her drive the 3.7 miles to the library (which included a left turn), although I did make her cut through the graveyard and go the back way across two parking lots. Yes, I admit I did get out of the car at the stop sign to make sure there weren't any trees or streetlights poised to hop out and block her view. And yes, on the way home I may have kept one hand on the door handle and the other in my mouth to stifle my screams, and both feet could have been locked on an imaginary brake pedal. Okay, I confess that when we got home it's possible I may have fallen prostrate on the driveway and sobbed a grateful thank-you to God that we arrived home in one piece. But I didn't, as Laura accused, "freak out." That would mean a loss of control, and if anything, I am in complete control.

Can You Say "Control Freak"?

I always knew I had controlish tendencies, but I would never come right out and call myself a "control freak." Other people are control freaks. I just know how things should be. I know the best way to do things, and I make it my goal to convey that information the best way I can to everyone around me.

Let's go back to Laura learning to drive. No, let's don't. I'm still having trouble prying my fingers from the car keys and relinquishing them to her. Let's talk instead about something less threatening, like Couch Rules. In my house the rules are simple: No sitting in the middle (because it causes the cushions to smush), and no body parts on the throw pillows.

Likewise, Bed Rules and Bathroom Rules are similarly simple. The bed pillows go in this order: First the plain dark green ones lean against the headboard at a slight angle, then the green floral pillows are placed slightly below the plain ones, then the cream eyelet ones (which are no-body-parts pillows). In the bathroom, the bath towels are to be folded lengthwise in thirds, then once over the towel bar and centered, with a no-body-parts hand towel on top. All bathroom towels are to be looked at only. Do not touch.

I realize some may see this as slightly, maybe even borderline, semicontrolling, but I assure you it is not. It's just that certain towels and pillows and sections of couches are clearly not to be touched. It's only right and proper.

I have other rules too. No cutting blocks of cheese crookedly. When one makes iced tea, one must not put spoonfuls of sugar into the pitcher. One must instead make a syrup of sugar and hot water so there won't be any wasted undissolved sugar at the bottom. Even distribution, I say.

I'm not controlling, but I do know exactly what topic Laura should use for her term paper and (even more exactly) how she should start it. I know what she should wear to school and how short/long she should wear her hair. I know that my husband needs to throw out that nasty shirt he wears to play softball in and that my mother should wear yellow and my sister shouldn't.

Of course, I almost never come right out and say anything, but I have my ways of getting my message across. I clear my throat a lot. Cough, nudge with my elbow. Point while pretending to scratch myself. Leave helpful notes, send encouraging e-mails. *I'm not trying to tell you what to do,* I might write, *but if I were you...* I especially like to send magazine articles or newspaper clippings with an added note: *Thought you'd enjoy reading this.*

But I'm not a control freak. Control freaks tell people what to do; I offer suggestions. Control freaks manipulate circumstances to suit their agenda; I lovingly and gently shape situations until they conform to the way they should be. Control freaks "freak out" when things don't go as they would like; I stay calm. I bite my lip, maybe clench my teeth. I might whimper, moan, pace the kitchen floor, slam a cupboard door or two. But I *don't* "freak out."

DRIVING ME CRAZY

The other day Laura asked if I would take her driving. Immediately my thoughts went to sideswiped mailboxes and dented garage doors. Not that she's done either. *But it could happen.* What if every moron, idiot, and jerk in a twenty-five-mile radius decides to drive down the exact street my daughter turns down and gets too close or cuts her off and I panic and scream, which makes her swerve into oncoming traffic? *It could happen.*

What if she makes a bad judgment? Since there's no brake pedal on the passenger side, I can't fix things. But, on the other hand, if I'm the one who always drives, if I never let her grow up and make her own decisions, if I keep her locked in her room on a Saturday night, if I keep nudging and pointing, coughing and suggesting, if I keep shaping circumstances and making up rules against body parts on pillows, then…what?

Frankly, I'm not sure what. I do know the whole thing drives me crazy because the more I try to keep order and control of everyone and every-thing around me, the more out of control I feel. More than anything, I hate feeling out of control.

So did Rebekah, Control Freak of the Bible. Maybe you know her story. Rebekah married Isaac, son of Abraham, and had twin sons, Jacob and Esau. She favored Jacob. Gave him extra cookies in his lunchbox. When it came time for school, she let Jacob do eeny-meeny to see which boy got the window seat in the car (which meant Jacob always won). She loved Esau, but there was just something about little Jakie.

The boys grew up and Dad got old. He was about ready to die when he decided he'd like some of that tasty stew Esau liked to make out of fresh wild game. Not that prepackaged low-fat meat substitute his wife fixed, trying to get his cholesterol level down. He wanted *meat*. So he sent for Esau and told him after he'd eaten some stew he would give his final blessing.

What they didn't realize is that Rebekah just "happened" to be listening to the conversation (that's what control freaks do), and went to work correcting the situation. She knew how things should be and if she didn't do something, well…she had to do something. So she told Jacob, "Look, Dad wants some of Esau's stew—and he also wants to pass on his blessing, which you and I know should be yours. This just won't do. Now, if I may make a suggestion, if you go out and bring me a couple of goat steaks from the freezer in the garage, *I'll* make Dad some stew just like he likes it. Then you bring it to him. Don't worry about a thing."

There was only one small hitch: how to make Isaac think Jacob was Esau. Rebekah paced the living room until Jacob came back inside the house. "Dad's almost blind, so he'll never know the difference," she told him. "We'll put some hair on you and you can wear your brother's hat and some of his aftershave. If your dad catches on, I'll take the heat. Just trust me. I'm your mother."

Things went as they should—that is, the way Rebekah planned. Isaac ate his stew, then blessed the wrong son (depending on your point of view). When Esau eventually came in and demanded a blessing from his father, Isaac didn't have one left. Instead, he only had words of a strife-filled future for his older son, which, to put it mildly, didn't sit well with the young man. Last anyone heard from Esau, he was vowing revenge on his conniving brother, muttering something about how Jacob should learn to sleep with his eyes open from then on.

Poor Rebekah. Things had not gone exactly as she'd anticipated. She had hoped they could all get along and that her favorite son would grow to be happy, fat, and sassy and remain by her side, maybe marry that nice girl down the street with the dimpled smile. She had hoped Jacob would give her dozens of grandchildren she could control (maybe one would be a doctor?), but she ended up having to send her favorite son away in order to save his life. Control-freak Rebekah had lost control. She lost the very thing she wanted to hold on to (Genesis 27, my paraphrase).

Several years ago Texas columnist Jeanie Miley wrote, "Controlling others may work for a time, but ultimately, control always fails. I may get by for a season playing one-up or even bullying others, but with control and power gone awry, there is always a day of reckoning and the scales *will* get balanced. If I must control other people, I will finally lose what I most want. Control freaks always lose control."

In the Genesis account of Rebekah's life, it doesn't say whether or not she ever saw her son Jacob again. Chances are she never did. What a pity. Control always fails. Love, on the other hand, never fails.

THE ORPHAN IS A DAUGHTER

The desire or drive to control stems from fear and insecurity. A woman held by fear controls because she is afraid no one else will take care of things. No one else can protect her family the way she can. No one else can get the job done. If she lets go, relinquishes control to someone else—even God—she might get hurt. Her children might make wrong choices, and they might get hurt or not reach their potential. Her husband might not be all that he should be if she didn't nudge, if she didn't do everything in her power to "shape" circumstances.

In her book *Tame Your Fears*, Carol Kent lists ten ways women exert control:

1. *The Manager.* She leads every group, is quick to volunteer, slow to delegate.
2. *The Manipulator.* This woman gets people to do what she wants and makes them believe it's their own idea; usually comes from a dysfunctional family.
3. *The Martyr.* Her motto: "No one else will do it." She controls with guilt and obligation.

4. *The Meanie.* She uses nagging, bullying, criticism, force.

5. *The Most Spiritual.* "I am the godly one and you are not. There-fore, my way (which is obviously God's way) is best."

6. *The Mother of the Extended Family.* This woman continues to "help" and "protect" her adult children, their spouses, her grand-children, etc. in order to keep them from making bad decisions.

7. *The Most Perfect.* She uses her own perfectionism and capability as a means of intimidation. "Who else can do it better?"

8. *The Mime.* She has perfected the look that says, "You'd better do it my way."

9. *The Morbid Weakling.* This woman uses her frailty, real or imag-ined, to be the center of attention. This ensures that everyone attends to her needs. Guilt is her favorite tool.

10. *The Main Attraction.* This is the woman who flirts with men in order to get what she wants from them.[1]

After reading Kent's list, I have to confess I've been guilty of most of those controlling behaviors at one time or another. However, it's not enough to know what I do or even why I do it. I need to know how to *stop.* How to unclench my fist around this need to be in control and let go.

Let go. By far the scariest two words in the English language for a per-son held by the need to control. The late Jack Miller used the phrase "act-ing like an orphan" to describe someone who is controlling. Among other things, orphans fend for themselves and take control of their surroundings. After all, if they don't, who will?

When that's my thinking, it's because I'm forgetting about my Father who loves me deeply, intimately, personally, care-fully, lavishly. Who loves me with an everlasting love and who draws me to himself with loving-kindness (Jeremiah 31:3). Who has taken away my punishment and calls me Daughter. My Father who delights in me and quiets me with his love. Who rejoices over me and sings love songs to me—about me (Zephaniah 3:14-17).

When I think I must be in control, I'm forgetting about my Savior who, though I once scoffed at his sacrifice, gave his life for me while I was yet in rebellion (Romans 5:8). My Savior who prays for me and pleads my case. My Savior who willingly trades my sin for his righteousness, my imperfection for his surpassing beauty. When I knock myself out trying to be in control, I'm forgetting that Jesus said he wouldn't leave me as an orphan (John 14:18), but promised to send me his Holy Spirit as my Comforter, Guide, Teacher, Source of power, and Friend.

When I forget that God is lovingly in control of my very life and breath—ultimately of everything in his universe—I get afraid. When I'm afraid, I cling to whatever I can to help me feel secure. I hold on to the illusion that I can control my own life. And in doing so, I drive myself and everyone around me crazy.

Control is not an idol I give up easily. Knowing it's worthless, knowing that it displeases the Lord and keeps me from experiencing freedom sometimes isn't enough to cause me to let go. I'm afraid to let go. But the Father loves me. Jesus prays for me. The Holy Spirit enables me. The perfect love of God casts out my fear and allows me to let go of my need to control. All I have to do is ask my Father to help me experience his love until I can let go. I ask of him, "Lord, help me let go of what I don't even hold in the first place."

Does it work? I thought you'd ask me that, so I tried it out—handed over the car keys to Laura and got in the passenger side. Without grimacing either. You would've been so proud. She did all right too. We made it to the store and back without an incident.

Okay, so what about tomorrow and the next day? I can't say right now. Like I told you, it's not easy. I guess the best I can say for now is that when tomorrow comes I'll have to ask my Father. For knowledge of his love, for help, for power, for grace.

After all, he said I could.

Think on These Things

1. If you could have complete control over any situation or person in your life, what or who would it be? How would you orchestrate things? What do you hope the outcome would be?

2. In her book *The Control Trap*, Barbara Sullivan calls fear "a trap we fall into, causing us to subtly or overtly take wrongful control of the lives of those around us." Name and describe controlling behaviors that stem from fear. Be honest: Which ones are you guilty of?

3. First John 4:18 in *The Living Bible* says, "We need have no fear of someone who loves us perfectly; [God's] perfect love for us eliminates all dread of what he might do to us. If we are afraid, it is for fear of what he might do to us, and shows that we are not fully convinced he really loves us." Think about the situation or person (from your answer to the first question) that you would like to control. How much of your desire for control stems from fear? How can you apply 1 John 4:18 to your own life?

4. Read Paul's prayer to the Ephesians (3:14-19). How have you experienced the love of God? As you consider the situation you would like to have control over, how does knowing God loves you change your thinking about it? How ready are you to *repent* of your control, *replace* it with God, and then *rejoice* in your freedom?

———————

O the deep, deep love of Jesus. Spread His praise from shore to shore!
How He loveth, ever loveth, changeth never, nevermore!
How He watches o'er His loved ones, died to call them all His own;
How for them He intercedeth, watcheth o'er them from the throne!
—Trevor Francis, "O the Deep, Deep Love of Jesus"

Chapter 9

The Virtuous Woman Meets Godzilla

Adam and Eve had an ideal marriage. He didn't have to hear about all the men she could have married, and she didn't have to hear about his mother's cooking.—Unknown

The longer I think about it, the more convinced I am that I could be a great wife and mother if it weren't for my family. Let's face it, they just aren't doing their parts.

Take my husband, for example. Barry's a terrific guy, don't get me wrong. But he has…quirks. He wears gray T-shirts and blue shorts. That's not a problem, but that's almost all he wears. He has his charcoal gray shirts and his lighter gray ones "for variety." His Hanes and his BVD's. All with varying degrees of threadbareness. Most look like they've been rubbed on a cheese grater—and that's how he likes them. I've offered to buy him other shirts in other colors and styles, but he likes what he likes.

In the winter (keep in mind, we live in Florida) he exchanges his blue shorts for jeans, but he keeps the gray T-shirts. He just adds a black sweatshirt. Has to be black. Or sometimes, just for variety, he'll put on a T-shirt that has a picture of a steam boiler on it. He has a drawer full of those that he gets from a boiler company he does business with. *He gives them as gifts.* If you come over to my house and Barry is there, chances are you'll go home with a steam boiler T-shirt. Everyone gets one. Or a steam boiler plastic cup.

A definite quirk.

Then there's his taste in music. The man is stuck in a time warp still waiting for the Dave Clark Five to make a comeback. His all-time favorite song is "Precious and Few." He hums *Chicago's Greatest Hits.* He calls Andy Williams "Moon River." Like, "Is Moon River still alive?" That's another one of his quirks. He's forever asking me if so-and-so is still alive. How would I know?

One day he came home from Home Depot with a free apron. He thought it rather manly, in an apronly sort of way. Just eight or so inches long. It was more like three big canvas pockets with ties around the waist. *He wore it for days.* He'd put his wallet in one pocket, his loose change in another and his coffee stirrers in the third. Then he'd tie it over his navy blue shorts and gray T-shirt (what else?) and…wear it. Everywhere.

Our daughters grew concerned. "Does Dad know he's wearing an apron?" Laura asked. Alison, a high school sophomore at the time, just pretended she was an orphan. I, on the other hand, couldn't pretend I was husbandless. Not that I wanted to. I mean, he's a good husband and all. He's just a husband who thinks wearing an apron is not odd. Unfortunately (heh-heh-heh) there was a tragic accident involving a can of paint and the poor unsuspecting piece of canvas. No one recalls exactly how it happened.

As I said before, I could be a great wife and mother if it weren't for my family. If I didn't have a husband who interrupts the crucial part of *Murder, She Wrote* to ask how to hard boil an egg, I wouldn't have to lose my cool and shoot "the look" at him during a commercial break. I wouldn't have to shake my head and tsk-tsk and be one of those judgmental sorts if he would share my political views. I wouldn't have to be a nag if he would just do things the right way the first time.

HER CHILDREN RISE UP?

The same goes for my kids. A few years ago I wrote a book about the Proverbs 31 woman. If you didn't read it, I'll give you the condensed version: She out-Marthas Martha Stewart. She's the epitome of perfection, and the average Christian woman either wants to emulate or flog her. I chose to emulate her and so set out to do everything the Scripture passage detailed her doing. Although I shouldn't have been, I was surprised that I kept failing. By the end of the book I discover that any virtue the Virtuous Woman has is Christ's virtue in her, and that, only by faith.

All this to say that, in my book, one of my favorite parts says, "Her children arise and call her blessed. Mine, upon arising, usually call me Mother (pronounced "Muh-therrrrrr!") and usually at the top of their lungs or in a high-pitched whine."[1] This brings me back to my original assertion that I could be a Great Mom if it weren't for my kids.

Actually, I have discovered the secret to perfect parenting: Keep them asleep. Of course, that only works with newborns and teenagers. Now that Alison is married and out of the house, I can safely say I am a Great Mom where she's concerned. As far as I know, she says and does everything correctly, follows my example as a wife, and flosses daily. Selective memory prohibits me from recalling any mistakes I may have made in raising her. As best I can remember, I did everything right with her. Even that matter of her running away to the driveway and hiding in the car the time I suggested she go to summer school wasn't due to any error on my part. I thought she would enjoy it. I always went to summer school as a kid. I didn't realize times have changed and now summer school is only for students who fail their classes. Other than that, I feel good about parenting Alison.

I could feel good about parenting Laura, too, if she would either (a) stay asleep, or (b) stop asking questions that can only be answered "Are you out of your mind?!"

She wanted to go to Daytona Beach with a friend. That in itself is not an unreasonable request. They wanted to leave after work on a Saturday night and stay until Sunday…with the friend's boyfriend coming too…and three other guys…and someone else's girlfriend…and they all wanted to rent one motel room and camp out…and all the friends were at least eighteen and Laura was only sixteen at the time.

I hate situations like that with all my heart, mind, body, and soul. I hate these requests and the "Why nots" that follow my "No way!"

"Why not, Mom? Everybody else is going. Don't you trust me? Why do you have to be so lame?! So what if everybody's eighteen. I'm almost eighteen! You used to be so cool, now you're such a…*mom.*"

At times like these all I want is for the ground to open up and swallow me whole. Instead, I grit my teeth and tell her that although mathematically eighteen minus sixteen is only two years (as she points out continuously, even in my dreams), those are dog years. Slow, tired, hound-dog years. On a good day, she'll change the subject and ask for something like a tattoo instead. Most times, though, she just hates me and gives me the loudest silent treatment you'd ever want to experience. She's furious—I'm furious. I'm furious because she's not following her script, the script that I've written where everyone does what they're supposed to and the spotlight is on me, center stage, in the starring role as the Most Virtuous Woman.

"TAKE 58,742: ACTION!"

My pastor-friend Ron Brown calls this the idol of the "perfect supporting cast." *It's not my fault. I'm the one with my lines memorized. I'm the one who knows my part. I know everybody else's part too. But they don't know their parts, and when I'm up on stage, they're making me look bad. And since I'm the star of the play, I'm the one who's going to get the bad reviews.*

Remember the idols test in chapter 1? (Is there a person, experience, possession, position, or relationship that if you can't have it you get angry, fearful, worried, or despondent?) I had told you that I'm rarely angry or despondent and that my idols mostly cause me to fear or worry. Not this one. My idol of the "perfect supporting cast" causes me to be cupboard-slamming, bad-word-thinking angry. I'm usually careful not to say what I think out loud, but I have to tell you, I've called my family members some terrible names inside my head. And as much as I hate to admit this, it's all my fault.

How I'd love to blame all my failures on anyone and everyone else for getting in my way of being the perfect spouse, parent, employee, friend, daughter, sibling. But I can't. Besides, who am I trying to fool? If anybody, I'm only fooling myself.

Of all my idols, this is one that hurts others more than it hurts me. When I blame others for my frustration over their shortcomings, even if I don't say a word, my body language screams the message, "*You're* the problem, not me!" It belittles and tears down, destroys my house like termites—or like a wrecking ball and crane.

I remember the early days of marriage and how I used to stand in the doorway of the bathroom in the mornings and watch Barry shave. I used to love watching my dad shave when I was a little girl. A machinist, my dad would shave with the same precision he used with his lathes and drill presses. Barry, not a machinist, didn't have that same exact precision my dad had in scraping shaving cream from his face. To me, he did it willy-nilly. Carelessly, I thought.

I remember feeling horrified. *What kind of animal did I marry?* I'd keep my distance from him and plan the best way to demand a divorce. ("Your Honor, I plead irreconcilable differences. My husband shaves incorrectly.")

I'd stand in the doorway morning after morning and try to telepathically send him the message, "You're doing it wrong! You're doing it wrong!" Finally one day I exploded. I yelled, "That's not how you're supposed to shave! That's not how my dad does it—why can't you do it right?!"

Fortunately, that didn't cause irreparable damage to my new husband's psyche. He more or less laughed it off and suggested I go home and marry my dad. However, it took me awhile to get over it. Mainly because it brought out character flaws in me that I had never been forced to deal with before. It's easy to be married when you aren't. When you're only thinking and dreaming about it, you only imagine yourself saying and doing the ideal. Even imagined arguments have you cast as Donna Reed playing opposite that charming doctor she had for a husband.

The same goes for motherhood. When you're pregnant, you know you're the best mother ever because that beachball of a belly contains the child who will do and say everything right. There's no doubt in your mind that you will respond according to everything the Bible and/or Dr. James Dobson says…until you're up at 3 A.M. for the fifteenth night in a row and you've been up since 5 A.M. the night before and all you want is for this kid to GO TO SLEEP!!! And you get mad at *her* for turning you into Godzilla incarnate. If it weren't for her, you'd be perfect in your role.

WHO IS THE STAR OF YOUR SHOW?

This summer I sat down to read the Gospels in *The Message*. Although I've read them many times over the past twenty-plus years, after a while the words become so familiar that I tend not to see them when I read. But with this version, every word was fresh and new.

One thing that struck me in this modern language account of the life of Jesus was how utterly cool Jesus was with people. He always said the coolest things and cut through all the garbage to get to the bottom line. For example, in his Sermon on the Mount, Jesus told his disciples:

Don't pick on people, jump on their failures, criticize their faults—unless, of course, you want the same treatment. Don't condemn those who are down; that hardness can boomerang. Be easy on people; you'll find life a lot easier. Give away your life; you'll find life given back, but not merely given back—given back with bonus and blessing. Giving, not getting, is the way. Generosity begets generosity.…

It's easy to see a smudge on your neighbor's face and be oblivious to the ugly sneer on your own. Do you have the nerve to say, "Let me wash your face for you," when your own face is distorted by contempt? It's this I-know-better-than-you mentality again, playing a holier-than-thou part instead of just living your own part. Wipe that ugly sneer off your own face and you might be fit to offer a washcloth to your neighbor. (Luke 6:37-38,41-42)

Ouch. But then Jesus also said, "When you pray, say, 'Father...'" He told his disciples to ask, seek, and knock and that the Father would meet their needs (and ours) and send the Holy Spirit. He told them that they (and we who believe) are no longer his servants and that we may call him "Friend." The prophet Isaiah called God our "Husband."

In my search for the perfect supporting cast, I mistakenly think I'm the star of the show. In reality, Almighty God is the star and I am the not-so perfect bit player. A walk-on. In light of that, what's left but to fall on my face and repent of wanting to be the ingenue and of throwing temper tantrums like a diva who blames her bad acting on everyone else in the play?

Okay, this is where my temperamental actress analogy breaks down. I was going to say, "Next I need to reread the script and follow the Director's commands"—but that only works in the theater. In real life, although we're only bit players, at the same time we're beloved children, friends, cherished brides. We don't merely follow the Director's command. Instead we cling tightly to the Director's hand, allowing his love to fill us to overflowing. We cry out to him to free us from the self-centeredness of our relationships so we can love others out of the abundance of his love for us. God is not only Director, but he is Maker, Husband, Savior, Brother, Friend. He is everything we want, everything we need, everything we search for.

The family of the Virtuous Woman of Proverbs 31 praised her as wife and mother, not because she had it all together but because she knew that the source of her soul's satisfaction was found only in God. It's written about her, "A woman who fears the LORD is to be praised" (v. 30).

May it also be said about you, and about me.

Think on These Things

1. If you are married: What were some of your expectations of marriage and children? Looking back, how realistic were they? If you're single: Describe your idea of the ideal relationship.

2. Read James 4:1-3. Take some time to dwell on each point of the passage and ask God to show you what needs to be done in your life in accordance with it. Do the same for James 4:6-10.

3. Proverbs 31 describes a virtuous woman or a "wife of noble character." The key to her character is found in verse 30. What does it mean to "fear the LORD"? (See Deuteronomy 6:5,12-14; Proverbs 8:13; Deuteronomy 10:12-21.)

4. If you are held by the idol of perfect relationships, how do the following scriptures help you to let go?

1 John 3:1-3

Jude 1

Psalm 68:5-6

Isaiah 54:5-6

Romans 15:13

---

*When people recognize God as the ultimate Significant Other,
they define their worth in terms of their relationship with him.*
—Tony Campolo, *The Success Fantasy*

Chapter 10

Confessions of a Pro...crastinator

Uh-oh. The light burned out.—Me, 1984

I think I've exceeded the record for staring at a roll of wallpaper: five days, three hours, and seventeen minutes. It's sitting on my kitchen table taunting me to hang it in the guest bedroom—the bedroom that's going to have guests in it in two days. I don't know what my problem is, it's just wallpapering a room...except, I've never done it before, and for some reason I can't seem to start.

Yesterday I decided I'd put it off long enough and spent the entire day at the library with the intention of reading wallpapering how-to books. Instead, I ended up reading *People* magazine and searching for my name on the Internet. (I'm not there.) Then I read about foot problems for forty-five minutes until it was time to pick Laura up from school. Now I'm back staring at that stupid roll of wallpaper, unable to take the first step.

Maybe it'll help if I grab some ice cream or watch TV for a few hours, I tell myself. *Or take a nap.* I check my watch, call a friend, wipe my finger through the dust on my china hutch. I eat a spoonful of ice cream, walk past the pile of clothes waiting to be ironed, then call another friend. I rearrange the items on my to-do list. I run out of friends to call. I sit back down at the kitchen table and agonize some more, and curse this affliction I suffer from, this inability to *just do it.*

THE NIGHT THE LIGHTS WENT OUT IN CALIFORNIA

I should've known I was in trouble when neither of my daughters' first words were *Mama* or *Dada*, but *later.* I should've known I had a problem when the warranty on the VCR expired before I even got around to hooking it up. Just like I should've known things had gone too far when I went to pick up my red wool slacks from the cleaners and discovered an exotic pets store had replaced the dry cleaner's six months earlier.

Since the experts say admitting you have a problem is the first step toward recovery, here goes: I am a procrastinator. My favorite day of the week is Someday. My favorite time of day is later. My motto is, "Why do today what you can put off until tomorrow?" I stood up and cheered during *Gone With the Wind* every time Scarlett O'Hara said, "I'll think about it tomorrow." I don't even bother with regular birthday cards, but head straight for the belated section. When I get around to it, I'm going to buy a supply of them to keep on hand. I may even mail them.

My life is filled with projects started and not completed. Pictures taken and film left undeveloped. Overdue library books stacked by the door. My lawn needs mowing, my windows need washing, and either I'm super early for Christmas or ten months too late and need to take the wreath off the front door. My poor houseplants keep dying because I never get around to watering them. The only reason my family is alive is because they can water themselves.

On the positive side, as a procrastinator I never make snap decisions that I might live to regret. I've perfected the wait-and-see attitude. It had to have been a procrastinator who coined the phrase, "If it ain't broke, don't fix it." I've taken it a step further and added, "Even if it *is* broken, leave it alone, since it will probably be obsolete in a few years anyway. Besides, throughout the ages man survived without having one in the first place." So, you see, procrastinating isn't completely a bad thing.

I've often thought about why I do it, usually when I'm trying to avoid something I should be doing, like wallpapering a bedroom. Maybe it's hereditary—everyone in my family procrastinates. It's the one trait we all have in common. We take pride in our procrastination. After all, we're pros, aren't we?

Growing up in a procrastinatory family, we had the only house on the block with Christmas lights up in June. We were raised thinking that paintings were supposed to sit on the floor, leaning against the wall. We didn't know bicycle flat tires could be fixed. We thought flashlights and transistor radios were disposable—nobody in our family *ever* bought batteries. But that's par for the procrastinator's course.

When I was ten, our family started saving pennies and nickels for a trip to the Grand Canyon. I'm forty-five years old. I haven't lived at home since I was nineteen. I have two kids of my own. One is married and the other is in high school. I *still* haven't gone to the Grand Canyon. And as far as I know, Mom still hasn't gotten around to cashing in our coins. Last time I talked to her she said that getting coin roll papers from the bank was number one on her list.

The list! That's the trademark of a true procrastinator. Every self-help book out to convert us into a non-pro lifestyle mentions making a daily list, the theory being that making a tangible to-do list motivates a procrastinator to actually *do*. Further thrills are promised with the crossing off of each accomplished task. *Ta-da!*

Au contraire. For the true procrastinator, the thrill comes from merely putting the task on the list in the first place. That way, we never really have to *do* anything. For example, if anyone asks, "Did you get the garbage disposal fixed?" we can whip out our list and reply, "Not yet—but it's *on my list!*"

Tops on my list: Replace refrigerator light bulb.

Truthfully, I didn't realize I had a problem with procrastination until Laura was three years old. One day she had come running home from the neighbor's house in a state of bewildered hysteria. It seems she had opened their refrigerator and was startled by the light. It's not as if our refrigerator didn't have a light. It's more like ours had burned out seven or eight years earlier and we just never got around to replacing it. (We still haven't.)

Once again, that's not necessarily a negative. I could argue that my procrastination has proven beneficial in that it has served to stimulate both daughters' curiosity and creativity over the years. If I had automatically replaced the light bulb, Laura might have missed discovering the contrast between darkness and light vis-à-vis refrigerators. If I had gone to the gas station as soon as I had put it on my list, Alison would have been denied the experience of running out of gas in the middle of the cauliflower field and of observing me kicking dirt all over the car. They wouldn't have known the joy of Christmas shopping in May for all the relatives. Or that one can live a normal, healthy life without a back porch light. (That one burned out too.)

I'm tempted to think I could even live happily ever after without wallpapering the spare bedroom, but something is nagging at me that it goes deeper than just wallpaper.

GOLD OR GARBAGE?

Burned out light bulbs, flashlights with dead batteries, undeveloped film, unmailed warranty cards—none of these threaten my sanity or quality of life. It's humanly possible to live without the wallpaper, so why does it have my stomach all in knots? It's only wallpaper.

But as I walk past the bedroom, my thoughts haunt me. *What if I fail? What if I do my best and it's not good enough? Maybe I just think I'm a better decorator than I really am. Everyone liked the dresser I refinished so much, they'll probably expect this project to be as good—or even better. Maybe if I keep putting it off I'll never have to face the real limits of my ability. Maybe I'll go get some more ice cream.*

I totally identify with Jane Burka who writes in her book *Procrastination: Why You Do It, What You Can Do About It,* "The fear of being judged as lacking ability is so powerful for some people that they would rather suffer the consequences of procrastination than the humiliation of trying and not doing as well as they had hoped. People who worry about being judged inadequate or unworthy usually are afraid that inadequate is exactly what they are."

I can't fathom doing less than a perfect job. For me, there's no middle ground. The thought of producing ordinary or average work is intolerable. Burka quotes one procrastinator as saying, "Either it's gold or it's garbage." However, for those of us who procrastinate because we're perfectionists, it's never gold. We keep setting our standards unreachably high, and instead of even trying, we usually end up watching marathon reruns of *thirtysomething.*

Take my wallpapering situation. I know it shouldn't be such a big deal. People wallpaper all the time and don't die from it. But...if I hang it wrong or it turns out crooked or the seams don't match, I will have failed.

I will *be* a failure.

Several years ago I had a phone conversation with Dr. Paul Meier, cofounder and medical director of the Christian-based New Life Clinics. As we talked about perfectionistic procrastinators, I remember telling him, "If I can't produce the best, then I don't want to even try."

I'll never forget what he told me. He said, "Your way of thinking is sin." Then he suggested (after I repented of my gold-or-garbage, unrealistic thinking) that I meditate on what Jesus said in Matthew 11:28-30. He told the people, "Come to me, all you who are weary and burdened, and I will give you rest. Take my yoke upon you and learn from me, for I am gentle and humble in heart, and you will find rest for your souls. For my yoke is easy and my burden is light."

Dr. Meier reminded me that we were created to live balanced, practical lives. What the Lord expects of us is easy, and his burden is light. In other words, if I am feeling overwhelmed and unable to keep up with the demands that I place upon myself, then I'm out of God's yoke, his will for me. What's worse, I'm setting myself higher than God in my expectations of myself. The Lord desires that I do everything as an act of loving worship to him, that I enjoy him and the gifts and talents he's given me. He's given me all the resources necessary to complete whatever he has put in front of me to do, whether it's my job, my relationships, my service to my church and community, my leisure, my wallpapering. I'm the one who says, "But that's not enough."

You would think by now I'd know that this excessive fear I have of being less than perfect could only mean one thing: yet another idol in my life. It seems like every time I turn around there's something else taking God's place. Once again the i-word is *self*. Rigid, self-imposed standards of what I think I should be and do to be acceptable in my own sight. Mistakenly I think that if what I do is perfect, then who I am must surely be perfect too. And if I'm perfect, then God will undoubtedly be pleased.

But I am wrong. God has never demanded that I be perfect, for he's the only perfect one. All he wants is for me to be his.

My Father's Shirt

The Bible tells me that nothing—neither life nor death nor other people's opinions of me, not even my own perfectionism and procrastination—can separate me from God's love. I may fail greatly at what I produce, but I'll never be a failure in God's eyes.

My pastor tells a story of a young girl who, while watching her older sister hang their father's white dress shirts on the clothesline to dry, decided she would like to do that too. However, she couldn't reach the clothesline. But she could reach the wheelbarrow. In her childlike naiveté and out of love for her daddy, she pinned one of his wet shirts on the rusty wheelbarrow handles. When her father came home and saw the shirt with the rust stains on it, he became enraged and punished his daughter severely.

While this story doesn't have anything to do with my perfectionism or procrastination, it has everything to do with God. My pastor goes on to say, "God as our Father doesn't treat us harshly for our failed attempts, neither does he merely overlook them. Our Father would take that shirt with the rust stains, put it on, and wear it to work. When someone pointed out the rust stains, he would smile and with great pride in his voice tell everyone, "My daughter laundered this shirt just for me because she loves me. Didn't she do a wonderful job?"

Max Lucado writes *In the Grip of Grace*, "God is for you. Had he a calendar, your birthday would be circled. If he drove a car, your name would be on his bumper. If there's a tree in heaven, he's carved your name in the bark. We know he has a tattoo, and we know what it says, 'I have written your name on my hand,' he declares (Isaiah 49:16)."

I'd like to add, if God had a spare room, he'd ask me to wallpaper it. And he would applaud my every effort. Even if I got the seams crooked and put the border on upside down. Besides, he would remind me, Christ is the only Perfect Wallpaper Hanger, and he has already credited his perfection to my account because of my faith in him.

Having reminded myself of that, I decide to confront my fears head-on and simply hang the wallpaper, just because it's something I've always wanted to do. Risk it all for the sheer pleasure of exercising my gifts for God's glory.

Then it dawns on me—"Whatever you do, work at it with all your heart, as working for the Lord, and not your houseguests" (Colossians 3:23, my paraphrase). I can do what's before me with all my heart and all my ability at the moment, and love will cover a multitude of wallpapering sins.

So I take the roll of wallpaper into the bedroom, take a deep breath, and begin. (That's the hardest part.) I make completion my goal instead of perfection. Finally, after a day and a half of smoothing and trimming and careful arranging of seams, I finish.

Is it perfect? *I don't know,* I tell myself, *perfect is such a relative term.* But I like it, I really do. And the room truly looks transformed.

You know, it's not the only one.

Think on These Things

1. In which areas of your life do you tend to procrastinate? On a scale of 1 to 10 (with 1 being mild and 10 being extreme), rate the negative effect your procrastination has on your quality of life (or on those around you!) in each area.

2. Some procrastination results from laziness or because a task has a low priority and so is relatively nonthreatening. However, procrastination in an area that you want to do well in usually stems from a fear of failure, success, or both. In the areas you mentioned in the previous question, go back and label each item with an *L* (laziness), *LP* (low priority), or *F* (fear). How can you apply the following scriptures to your items labeled *F*?

    Psalm 73:26

    Psalm 37:4-6

    Galatians 5:1

    2 Corinthians 3:17

3. Striving for perfection is not the same as pursuing excellence. Perfectionism is a compulsion toward unrealistic goals and a beating up of yourself when you make a mistake. List some worthy goals Christians should set for themselves. (Bonus question: What is the difference between perfection and excellence?)

4. Perfectionism is a form of *self*-righteousness. In what ways might Christians try to earn favor with God through perfectionism? How would the following scriptures help a perfectionist to relax and "just do it"?

Romans 8:31-39

2 Corinthians 12:9

Ephesians 3:20

Philippians 1:6

Colossians 3:23

It is a snare to imagine that God wants to make us
perfect specimens of what he can do;
God's purpose is to make us one with himself.
—Oswald Chambers, *My Utmost for His Highest*

Chapter 11

A Star Is Born

"If anybody wants to clap," said Eeyore, "now is the time to do it."
They all clapped.
"Thank you," said Eeyore. "Unexpected and gratifying, if a little lacking in
Smack."—Eeyore, The House at Pooh Corner

This is a little-known fact about me, and even though you haven't asked, I'll tell you anyway: I am royalty. At least I've always thought of myself as a princess. From the time I could raise my imaginary scepter and adjust my own crown upon my head and scream, "Look at me, everybody!" I've sought the limelight. "Holding court" as my dad used to call it.

I was truly an adorable child, and I surrounded myself with people who shared the same opinion. If you wanted to be my friend, you had to applaud my every effort. And being a benevolent princess, I gave my subjects plenty of opportunities for applause. Whenever I'd do something especially noteworthy (in my opinion), I'd cue the fanfare and insure that all eyes were on me. It's the applause that counts, you know.

I've never had a tapeworm, and I don't plan to any time soon, but I imagine the love of applause is tapewormish. Tapeworms are carnivores and keep growing inside a person until they eventually take over. But since the thought of that makes me squeamish, I think I'll change the subject and tell you about my award-winning performance in the starring role as Emily in *Our Town* in Mrs. Melke's eighth-grade drama class at Christopher Columbus Junior High School in Canoga Park, California.

I was brilliant. Never had there ever been a more perfect Emily in the history of Christopher Columbus Junior High School, or probably in all of Canoga Park. Maybe even the Western Hemisphere. At the auditions—I can't remember the name of the girl who tried out against me, although I can still see her long brown hair done in braids just for the auditions—I won hands-down. She looked more like Emily than I did (at that time I wore my short hair teased in a bubble, with bangs hanging in my eyes, and I wouldn't have been caught dead without my black eyeliner and white Yardley Slicker lipstick). However, I had the dreamy, faraway look and dreamy, ethereal, almost British "I'm ready to go back now" down perfectly. Thornton Wilder surely rolled over in his grave at the sound of my recitation. Truly, a star was born that day.

Opening night drew a standing-room-only crowd of at least thirty people in our little drama classroom. *Thornton Wilder's* Our Town *starring Nancy O'Brand as Emily...and some other people are in it too.* I acted my hammy, glory-seeking thirteen-year-old heart out that night, and after it was all over, the accolades from my adoring fans and the handwritten note of praise from the girls' assistant vice principal caused me to fall head over heels in love with the sound of applause. (As long as the applause is for me, that is.)

My junior high school stage career was short-lived. By ninth grade it interfered with my pursuit of Bob Richardson. Nevertheless, I had tasted the limelight, and it tasted delicious.

TAKE A BOW

You'll be happy to know that now that I am older and wiser, I'm no longer a princess. Now I am Queen. Basically it's the same thing, except now I seek applause from much larger audiences.

A few years ago when my first book came out, I started getting invitations to speak. At first I turned them down because I'd never done it before. But then I decided God was calling me and I must obey. Besides, a fan letter now and then, a favorable book review here and there, an occasional note from a friend telling me how absolutely brilliant I am—as nice as they were, they just weren't doing it for me anymore. I wanted, I *needed* more. I needed to know someone saw, someone approved. Someone loved and adored me. Clapping loudly helped too.

I remembered Mrs. Melke's eighth-grade drama class and how I felt having all eyes on me, everyone hanging on my every word (or so I thought), in total awe of ME. I remembered the applause and wanted it again. So in response to the call of God on my life, I started accepting speaking engagements.

That's when I discovered something better than applause: laughter. I made people laugh! They laughed *and* applauded! I knew God had done the right thing in calling me to speak to women on his behalf. I knew by the responses I got. Again, you would be amazed at how good I got at accepting the praises heaped upon me.

But as high as the heaps would get, they were never quite high enough. The laughter was never boisterous enough. No one guffawed at anything I ever said, as far as I can recall. I'd remember a guffaw. Or a chortle. No, they mostly twittered, although one lady did have Diet Pepsi come out her nose. But I prefer rolling-on-the-floor, side-holding, air-gasping laughter. And spontaneous applause interspersed throughout my talk. Standing ovations are nice too.

See, if people applaud, then I must be worth something. Unfortunately, for some reason the crowds I spoke to started lacking an appropriate appreciation of me. Not only that, the crowds soon became not nearly large enough.

And then I hit The Big Time.

I'd met a woman who pastored a church. She had come to one of my book signings, and after having recognized me as a Star, she issued an invitation to speak at her church. *Of course* I said yes.

We made all the arrangements and I rented a car, since mine is a pile of bolts held together by ten years' worth of kids' spit-out gum (and, therefore, not a vehicle worthy of a Queen). Her church is in a large city (compared to my town), and she told me she had advertised my appearance on two radio stations, plus TV. "If the crowd is too big, would you mind speaking at two services?" she asked me one day over the phone.

I envisioned people lined up around the block—women, children, small animals, and large men—all waiting to hear me speak, all eager to give me the attention and honor I craved. As I put my rental car in drive and headed toward Gainesville, I didn't know what to expect, other than a mob of people waiting to see me. After all, my appearance had been advertised on TV and radio all over the city.

The weather was perfect that day, a crisp, clear December Saturday. It was as if God had designed the day just for me, a day fit for…well, for a Queen. I found the church without a problem. It was the one with the hand-lettered sign in the window of a storefront building and a homeless man sitting out front. The buildings on either side of the church had bars on the windows and looked abandoned. At least I could make my way through the crowd with ease, all seven of them, including the homeless man who came inside once the doors were opened to get out of the cold and eat cookies.

It was as if God had designed the day just for me.

As you've probably already guessed, only one service was needed to accommodate the crowd. They listened attentively and laughed and applauded at the appropriate moments. The homeless man asked if I would read a poem he had written, and a woman whose husband was a Muslim and an important man in the community cried. Somehow, despite all my self-serving babbling, God had touched her.

Afterward the pastor asked everyone to show their love and appreciation to me "with hearts full of generosity," and they did. They passed a basket and gave me a small fortune: $28. Then they laid hands on me and prayed a blessing on my life. Never had the applause been more deafening.

THE APPLAUSE OF HEAVEN

Since I'm being honest, I want you to know that I've never done anything unselfishly or without thoughts of *Who will see me?* Never. Not even once in my whole, entire life. I did, however, come close last Christmas when my neighbor went out of town and asked me to feed her dog.

She's a single mom with two small children, and when I stopped by to feed her dog, I noticed her house needed cleaning. So one morning I went over there with my bucket, my scrubber sponges, and bottle of sudsing ammonia and thoroughly cleaned every inch of her kitchen—even the inside of the refrigerator. I had the best time doing it too.

But she didn't notice. Or if she did, she didn't say anything to me about it. You're going to have to trust that I'm telling you the truth when I say it was okay. On a scale of one to ten, it bothered me only about a one's worth. Hallelujah, I'm making progress! (Of course, when my neighbor reads this and recognizes it's about her, I'm sure she'll call and thank me profusely for cleaning her kitchen. She might even bring me a cake as a belated thank-you gesture.) It seems that although I may be making progress, I still have a long way to go.

I wasn't going to tell you this, but yesterday at the newspaper I work for, my story on page 3A was picked as "best read of the day." Every day at two o'clock the newspaper staff meets, and we go through that morning's paper and discuss what's good and what needs improvement. At the end of the meeting we choose the day's best story, headline, and photo. The reason I'm telling you this is *not* so you will be duly impressed and secretly wish you could be like me (although I wouldn't stop you if you wanted to think that). No, I'm telling you because my story in today's paper *wasn't* chosen. Wasn't even mentioned.

Now that's happened lots of times before, but with this particular story (about comfort foods) I used clever words like *noodly* and *slurp*. When I woke up this morning and ran out to get the paper from my driveway, all I could think about was getting "best read of the day" two days in a row. I remember thinking that it might even be a first in the history of that newspaper for a reporter to get it two days in a row. All day, I couldn't wait for the two o'clock meeting, especially since the high I felt from being chosen the day before had long worn off.

I don't remember whose story was chosen today, just that mine wasn't even mentioned. No one applauded. No one even noticed how cleverly I had used the word *slurp*.

I felt unsettled. Uneasy. Disconcerted. I pounded the keys to my computer and spun around in my chair. I sensed that God was trying to tell me something, but the thoughts of anticipated-yet-not-received applause drowned him out.

Later, on my way home, I heard him. Only he wasn't saying the things I'd imagined he'd say. Things like, "You shouldn't expect people to applaud your every effort" or "Grow up" or "Too much honey will make you sick." He didn't even say, "If you're praised here on earth, then you've already received your reward and there won't be anything waiting for you in heaven."

Instead, I think I heard God chuckle. I think he laughed with enjoyment over the way I used *slurp* and *noodly*. I think he said *he* noticed and that he thought it was a "best read of the day." I think he told me that he remembered the fun I had cleaning my neighbor's kitchen and that he had fun watching me too. That he sees everything I do, even when no one else does. And that whatever I do in his name, he applauds. He cheers for me. He roots for me. He wears a button on his lapel with my picture on it. He looks down from heaven and says, "That's my kid!"

Want to know something odd? It's not the condemning words that go through my head that drive me to repent of my love of the limelight; rather, it's knowing that God claps for me that brings me to my knees. It's God's kindness, wrote the apostle Paul, that leads to repentance (Romans 2:4).

God allows me to wander so I'll feel lost; he lets me seek attention everywhere else until I know I'll never be satisfied by anything other than him, and then he whispers in my ear, "I see what you do, and I'm pleased." For when I hear the applause from heaven, I'm reminded once again that

I'm a princess after all, and that my Father the King is pleased with me. Knowing that, why would I want anything less?

Think on These Things

1. Think about the last compliment you received. What was it for? How did it make you feel? How do you usually respond when someone gives you a compliment?

2. When was the last time you thought you deserved recognition but didn't receive any? How did you react?

3. The Christian life is a paradox: The first shall be last; the greatest is the one who is servant of all. In thinking about the idol of attention, what do the following scriptures say about a paradoxical life?

    Matthew 5:14-16

    Matthew 6:1-4

    Matthew 6:16-18

    Matthew 6:19-21

4. How do the following scriptures help someone who is held by a need for attention?

Philippians 2:3-4

Philippians 4:19

Psalm 149:4-5

Ephesians 2:1-10

Matthew 25:21

———————

Our deepest passion for significance is finally satisfied
when we realize he is all we need and we are "somebody" to him.
—Carol Kent, *Secret Longings of the Heart*

Chapter 12

He Never Promised You a Rose Garden

That's the difference between me and the rest of the world.
Happiness isn't good enough for me. I demand euphoria!
—Calvin of Calvin and Hobbes

When it comes to theology, I am definitely a Calvinist. (That's Calvin as in the comic strip character from *Calvin and Hobbes*.) Calvin believes the world revolves around him, and his highest goal in life is to wear rocket ship underpants and be euphoric. A wad of gum in his mouth and a loaded water balloon in his hand make him happy. He lives for leisure and chafes at rules. If he could, he would spend the rest of his life making philosophical statements on society through the construction of macabre snowmen. When presented with a choice, Calvin weighs his options carefully, then goes with whichever one suits his fancy at the moment.

Except for the rocket ship underpants, that's basically how I live my life too. I, like Calvin, want to be happy.

Maybe you've heard the southern saying, "If Mama ain't happy, ain't nobody happy." It's one of my favorite sayings. First of all, I like saying *ain't*. (It makes me happy.) Second, since I truly want others around me to be happy, it's good to know that the way to accomplish that is to make myself happy first. For the good of others, it's a sacrifice I'm willing to make. Besides, it fits nicely with my Calvinist principles of looking out for my own best interests.

I remember a time back in junior high school when I decided a surprise party for my birthday would make me happy beyond words. My birthday's in December, so in October I started dropping hints to all my friends. Not known for my subtlety, I'd pass notes in class to my friend Cheryl Peterson that said, "Only forty-three days until Nancy's birthday. Plan her surprise party *now*." I let everyone know which Beatles records I didn't have, whom to invite (Bob Richardson and Scott Kelly were two definite musts) and whom *not* to invite (Garrett "the Carrot" Parkinson).

Maybe my friends loved me, or maybe I wore them down with all my "hinting." Maybe even back in seventh grade God was orchestrating the events of my life and answered my request but sent leanness to my soul as he did with the Israelites who whined for meat instead of manna. Whichever was the reason, I arranged to be out of the house at the proper party-guest-arriving hour. I don't remember where I went or what I did, but knowing me the way I do, I imagine I went someplace with a mirror so I could practice looking surprised.

At the proper guest-of-honor-returning time, I walked into my house, and as per my instructions, all my friends leaped out and yelled, "Surprise!" *Of course* I feigned surprise (after all, I had been practicing), but *of course* I wasn't. Not only wasn't I surprised, but the party didn't make me as ecstatically happy as I had supposed it would.

Oh sure, it was fun when we dumped Kentucky Fried Chicken gravy on a neighbor's driveway, rang the doorbell, then when they came outside, Garrett the Carrot (they invited him anyway) pretended to throw up and we all ran away. It was fun tossing each other into the pool with our clothes on and playing kissing games and gossiping about whoever wasn't there, but it didn't make me happy beyond words. No euphoria—what a ripoff! I had gotten what I thought I wanted, but...

So I decided what would make me so happy I would never want anything else as long as I lived was a pair of white go-go boots like the dancers wore on *Hullabaloo*. At the Stride Rite shoe store where my mother bought my orthopedic saddle shoes every year when I was in elementary school, they had a pair of white go-go boots in the window. Since I had long outgrown the need for orthopedic shoes, I begged my mother to let me get a pair of those boots. I envisioned myself frugging and watusi-ing and jerking all over school in my psychedelic minidresses, fishnet stockings, and official white *Hullabaloo* go-go boots. I would be one swingin', groovy, *happy* chick.

Because God probably couldn't pass up the chance for me to be the grooviest girl at Christopher Columbus Junior High School, Mom just happened to have a full buy-twelve-pairs-of-shoes-at-the-regular-price-and-get-one-pair-free card. All those years of orthopedic saddle shoes were about to pay off.

I was right, too. They were groovy boots. But I only wore them once, and not even to school. I don't know why. I guess I just didn't like them as much on me as I did on the *Hullabaloo* dancers.

The same thing happened with the next pair of shoes I bought. They had "real French heels," and I got them at Thom McAn. I had seen a high school girl in my neighborhood wearing them and since she looked happy, I got some too. I wore them a few times, then put them in the back of my closet. Another ripoff.

THE TRUTH HURTS

I could probably go on for a hundred pages telling you all about how I've pursued happiness but never completely captured it, but I'm sure you have similar stories. We all do. Not even Calvin in his rocket underpants ever completely captures happiness. As he says, "What good is wearing rocket underpants if no one ever asks to see them?" Or as the late Gilda Radner used to say, "It's always something." There's always a fly in your pudding, a glitch in the works.

I'm doing my best to avoid what I need to say next, but there's no getting around it. I have a friend who recently told me, "I'd give up everything I own if I could just be happy. I *deserve* happiness!" Although I love my friend and would like nothing more than to see her happy, I cringed at her words. The cold, hard truth is we don't deserve happiness, and God never promised it to us. I wish I could make that sound less harsh, but I can't. As my brothers used to taunt after one of them said something painfully honest (yet for them, enjoyably brutal), "The truth hurts!"

The truth is, one of the most insidious idols we all have is the idol of personal happiness. (I'm being bold here and making a generalization by saying "we all" because I have a strong hunch that God will agree.) It's basic. Nobody wants to be *un*happy.

Happiness, however, is a relative term. What makes me happy might not make you happy. Or it might take more to make me happy than it does to make you happy, or vice versa. Not only that, happiness is slippery. Just when you think you've grasped it, it slides right out of your hands. Or it's like a house of cards. Tenuous. Totally dependent on just the right circumstances to keep it from toppling over.

For example, say you're having a great day. Nobody has gotten mad at you; Cinnamon Toast Crunch cereal is on sale for two dollars a box. The males in your household put the toilet seat down every time, and the females (including you) didn't throw any hissy fits. The mailman brought a magazine and a letter from a friend, but no bills. Someone asked if you've lost weight and you discovered a twenty-dollar error in your checkbook—in your favor.

All is well; life is swell…until you go to start up your car and it makes heaving sounds until it throws up antifreeze all over the driveway—and it's your turn to drive afternoon carpool and there are five middle schoolers waiting for you to pick them up, and one has soccer practice and has to be home extra early today. After you cry and kick your tires or use words you usually punish your kids for saying, you forget about how happy you've been all day and only think about your miserable existence. *Oh, woe is you.*

See what I mean by tenuous? Happy one minute then *Poof!* licking dust the next.

Or maybe you had a happy childhood and assumed adult life would be a continuation of the same. *And I lived happily ever after.* You married your high school sweetheart who took your breath away with his sweetness and charm. But something happened on the way to *ever after.* Sweet Prince Charming turned into a toad, or even the Big, Bad Wolf. You're not happy, and you can't even remember the last time you were. Now it's all you ever think about. *I just want to be happy. Surely God wants that for me too.*

You plot and plan. You daydream and remember. You start every thought with "if only." *If only I were married to someone else. If only I had a bigger house, newer car, whiter teeth, straighter hair. If only I had a different job, more money, fewer kids, a darker tan. If only I could play tennis. If only I could sing. If only...if only...if only. If only...then I would be happy.*

Next thing you know you're thinking things you know you shouldn't, planning things you know are wrong. Or maybe they're not wrong, just not good. Not best. You try to find happiness anywhere and any way you can.

As an idol, happiness is more like a bunch of idols rolled into one. As my thinking goes, *If only my family were perfect, I had control of my surroundings, had Winona Ryder's nose, and owned everything in the Chadwick's of Boston catalog...if only I could eat anything I want and not gain weight, have everything I attempt turn out perfectly, and have people adore me, then I would be...*

The truth is, I would still be "chasing the wind," as King Solomon called it. He should know; he had it all: money, power, sex, honor, *stuff.* Anything you and I could ever want, he had, yet he still wasn't happy. He wrote, "I thought in my heart, 'Come now, I will test you with pleasure to find out what is good.' But that also proved to be meaningless" (Ecclesiastes 2:1). He tried cheering himself with wine and undertook great projects. He built houses and planted vineyards, gardens, and parks. He owned slaves and herds and flocks, amassed fortunes, and became greater than anyone.

> I denied myself nothing my eyes desired; I refused my heart no pleasure. My heart took delight in all my work, and this was the reward for all my labor. Yet when I surveyed all that my hands had done and what I had toiled to achieve, everything was meaningless, a chasing after the wind; nothing was gained under the sun. (Ecclesiastes 2:10-11)

HAPPINESS OR BLESSEDNESS?

If not even Solomon, the man who had everything, could find lasting happiness, then what chance is there for you or me? The answer, of course, is none. No chance. Like I said before, God didn't promise us happiness and ease or a lifetime of pleasure. He did, however, say that if we are in relationship with him through faith in Christ, we will be blessed.

In the *Amplified Bible,* that word *blessed* is translated "blithesome, joyous, fortunate, and spiritually prosperous with life-joy and satisfaction in God's favor." It's a dancing in the street, singing in the rain, laughing through tears, unmovable, unshakable, deep-seated joy. Not dependent on any thing, person, or circumstance other than our connection with the Father.

In his Word to us, from Genesis to Revelation, God shouts, "You are blessed!"

Blessed…to be fruitful and multiply. (Genesis 1:22)

Blessed to plant and reap a hundredfold. (Genesis 26:12)

Set apart by the Lord…and blessed this day. (Exodus 32:29)

Blessed in all the work of my hands. Blessed with protection over my journey. (Deuteronomy 2:7)

Blessed with his presence. Blessed…and lacking nothing. (Deuteronomy 2:7)

Blessed with God's correction when I'm wrong. (Job 5:17)

Blessed with refuge. (Psalm 2:12)

Blessed with forgiveness. (Psalm 32:1)

Blessed because I make the Lord my trust. (Psalm 40:4)

Blessed because I've set my heart on pilgrimage…and find my strength in him. (Psalm 84:5)

Those who fear the Lord are blessed. (Psalm 112:1)

Blessed because my help is the God of Jacob…and my hope is in the Lord. (Psalm 146:5)

Blessed when I find wisdom. (Proverbs 3:13)

Blessed when I listen to it. (Proverbs 8:34)

Blessed when I am kind to the needy. (Proverbs 14:21)

Blessed when I wait for the Lord. (Isaiah 30:18)

Blessed when I maintain justice and do right. (Isaiah 56:1-2)

When I am poor in spirit, I am blessed. When I mourn over my sin, put on Christ's meekness, and hunger and thirst for the righteousness of God, I am blessed. Because God blesses me, I am merciful and pure in heart. I am a peacemaker—a blessing to my neighbors as I share the Good News of reconciliation between a holy God and sinful people. I am blessed even when I am persecuted for righteousness' sake. When I do what's right and everyone laughs. When I'm thought of as a Jesus Freak, *I am blessed.* (Matthew 5:3-12)

Because I have not seen Christ with my eyes or touched his face with my hand, yet have believed, I am blessed. (John 20:29)

Those who have faith are blessed. (Galatians 3:9)

Those who persevere are blessed—and those who are blessed persevere. (James 1:12)

Those who are invited to the wedding supper of the Lamb, whose sins are forgiven, who have received a new name, a new nature, a new heart…are blessed. (Revelation 19:9)

It doesn't matter whether my life is going smoothly or I'm curled up in pain, I am still blessed. When I have more than enough and my relationships work, when I'm stricken with grief or dying from loneliness, *I am still blessed.* No matter what my situation or circumstances, God blesses me with his presence. He has taken away my punishment and turned back my enemy. He quiets me with his love and even rejoices over me with singing. (Zephaniah 3:15-17)

"That's nice," you say. "Thank you very much for telling me all that, but…" But you're *still* not happy. (My, my, you're stubborn!) Well, let me tell you this: I don't know why God does what he does. I don't know why some people's lives are hard and others aren't. I don't know why God doesn't seem to answer your prayers, why your husband is a jerk and your neighbors harass you. I only know that "those [you?] who cling to worthless idols [like the pursuit of personal happiness] forfeit the grace [the experience of the freedom we have in Christ] that could be theirs" (Jonah 2:8). I know that repentance brings release, and release brings about freedom, and freedom causes one's soul to rejoice.

"Blessed are those who have learned to acclaim you, who walk in the light of your presence, O LORD," wrote the psalmist. "They rejoice in your name all day long; they exult in your righteousness. For you are their glory and strength" (Psalm 89:15-17).

Correct me if I'm wrong, but that sounds like happiness to me.

Think on These Things

1. On a scale from 1 to 10 (with 10 being extremely happy and 1 being extremely unhappy), how would you rate your life in general? What makes you happy? What makes you unhappy?

2. When you are feeling unhappy, what thoughts go through your head? (Be honest.) Read Psalm 42. Go over it and list all the references to feelings of sadness. Now go over it again and list all the words of hope and encouragement. Try this with other psalms, too, such as 40 and 86. (Bonus: Write your own psalm or prayer. Don't be afraid to put down your unhappy thoughts as well as your praise.)

3. On a piece of paper, make a "three *R's*" chart *(repent, replace, rejoice)*. Under each heading write down your thoughts concerning your pursuit of personal happiness. Be specific. What does it mean to repent of this idol? What aspect of God's nature or which specific area of his blessing can you replace it with? How will you rejoice?

––––––––––

*The settled happiness and security which we all desire God withholds from us
by the very nature of the world; but joy, pleasure and merriment
He has scattered broadcast. We are never safe, but we have plenty of fun,
and some ecstasy. It is not hard to see why. The security we crave would
teach us to rest our hearts in this world and pose an obstacle to our return to
God: a few moments of happy love, a landscape, a symphony, a merry
meeting with our friends, a bath or a football match, have no such tendency.
Our Father refreshes us on the journey with some pleasant inns,
but will not encourage us to mistake them for home.*

—C. S. Lewis

Chapter 13

Score One for the Home Team

All things being equal, you lose. —Anonymous

When I sat down to plan this book, I carefully chose which idols I would include. When it comes to this one, the idol of winning and being right, I specifically chose it thinking, *At last! Here's one I don't have a problem with!* This idol has to do with pettiness, competition in relationships, "keeping score," always having to be right, getting in the last word, etc. I thought I could use this chapter to send concealed messages to people I know who actually do have this as an idol in their lives.

But then God had to go and do what God does best, namely reveal my sin to me just when I think I'm doing okay.

In a book I picked up at the dentist's office, right in the first chapter it asked "Are You Addicted to Being Right?" Being the very subject I wanted to write about, it caught my attention. A gift from God to help me in my research! How kind of the Lord to help. Naturally I took the test with other people in mind. Here are some of the questions:

- Would you rather be right than happy?

- Is being right the foundation for your relationships?

- Do you have to have the last word in an argument?

- Do you find yourself discussing disagreements long after they are finished, just to prove you were right?

- Does proving your point of view take precedent over listening to others?

- Even after being demonstrated wrong, do you still search for ways to prove your point of view?

- Is your opinion more important than fact?

- Does being right feel crucial?

- If you admitted you were wrong, would it shock people around you?[1]

I don't want to tell you how I scored. Just know I'm feeling a bit squirmy right now. I was so sure I didn't have a problem in this area! *Rats.* Well, rather than deal with my idolatry, my so-called addiction to Being Right (and then having to think about repenting and changing and being free to be wrong), I'll tell you about some other people and their idolatry. That always makes me feel better about myself.

WHAT'S THE SCORE?

I have a friend who is newly married. (I promised her I wouldn't use her real name, so I'll call her Sue.) She's the scorekeeper in their marriage. When I knew I wanted to write about this subject, she's the first person I thought of. (Don't worry about this offending her. She knows she's a mess, and she's hoping someday she'll get tired of keeping score and let God free her. But she's not ready yet.)

Anyway, I asked her to explain her point system and how she manages to keep track of the score. This is what she said:

"First of all, everything has points, which I make up as the situations arise. For instance, if Steve* takes out the trash, that's worth one point, sometimes two. If he does it without me having to ask, I might give him a bonus point or I might not, depending on how I feel at the time.

"If he falls asleep on the couch, that might be a negative point. *But,* if he's been on my nerves and he falls asleep and I get to play on the computer or read a magazine without him interrupting me to help him find his favorite cup—which is *always* in the same place—then he might get five or six points. But if I want to go someplace and he falls asleep on the couch, then that's about a negative seven."

Sue went on (and on and on and on) saying, "It's really hard to think of examples of petty winning and losing because that's just my life—and I almost always win. Steve is easily bribed and is really good at giving in to my demands. I don't necessarily keep score—it's not like I write everything down—I just have a *very* good memory. Like, he still owes me for baking a batch of cookies on short notice for the bake sale at work that he signed up for and forgot to tell me about. All I want is for him to mow the lawn and bring in the towels after he uses them to wash the car. Oh, and when he cooks something, I'd like him to clean up the mess. So, until he does…I win. Right?"

Part of me wants to laugh and feel superior as I listen to Sue tell me about her scorekeeping. I mean, it is petty, and she knows it. It's destructive and silly, and it doesn't make her happy. Neither does it get her what she wants. (She wants to be Queen of Everything.) Part of me does laugh—she laughs too when she tells me. But there's a deeper part that knows I do the same things in my relationships. However, other people's pettiness is much more amusing than my own. It's a lot easier to laugh when it's someone else's sin.

*Not his real name.

ADDICTED TO BEING RIGHT

You know what really irks me? When people use the word *anxious* when they mean to say *eager*. When someone says, "I'm anxious to go to Disney World on Saturday," I practically bite my lip to keep from screaming, "No—unless you have an overwhelming fear of Mickey Mouse and are dreading the thought of a visit to the Magic Kingdom, you're EAGER, not anxious!" Whenever people tell me they're anxious to do something when I know they're looking forward to it (and therefore *eager*), a feeling of Rightness comes upon me. I am Right and the person is Wrong. The person is *wrong*. I'm right—you're wrong. Winner (me). Loser (you).

I suppose I should warn you: If you ever meet me in person and we have a conversation, be prepared to have only the second to the last word because I have the last word. Always. (That's because I'm Right.) Also, be prepared to have me correct you when you're wrong. It's just a little public service gesture I like to offer. But don't worry. I'm so good at it, you will hardly notice that I'm tearing you down (or at least adding to your limited knowledge on a subject) in order to build myself up.

So you'll know what to expect, here's how it will look: You'll say something like, "It's a nice day out." Then I will inform you that there's a 60 percent chance of rain and that Hurricane Zelda is expected to hit by morning. Or you'll tell me, "I went to see *Cats* on Broadway last month." To which I will add, "I heard they originally wanted to call it *Skunks*." I won't ever make anything up (other than that skunk thing just now), but I won't let anything slide by, either, without adding my two cents' worth. It's the Right thing to do, you know.

Normally I don't have a problem with my Rightness. (That's because I'm almost always Right.) Occasionally I run into someone who thinks he or she is right, however, and then we have a Situation. Usually I avoid Situations. I don't like turmoil and chaos or arguments unless I know I can win. If I think I can't, then I will keep silent and be satisfied with my inner

Rightness. Sometimes, however, Situations arise and I have no choice but to fight to the death. Better to die Right than admit to being Wrong.

Although my selective memory keeps me from recalling much of my past Situations, one stands out in my mind. I was fifteen or sixteen and in the kitchen making homemade pizza with my dad. I don't remember what I was so steadfastly Right about other than it was either putting the cheese on before the meat or the meat before the cheese.

All I remember is arguing with my dad until it escalated into a one-way screaming match. (I screamed while Dad kept putting meat—or cheese—on the pizza.) I remember the fury I felt and the absolute conviction that I. Was. Right. *I was Right!* I don't remember if Dad sent me to my room or if I stormed off on my own accord, just that I spent the rest of the night crying on my bed.

The irony is, after the first few seconds of our cheese-first/meat-first debate, I wasn't as absolutely sure of my convictions as I had made it sound. In fact, once my dad explained why his way was correct (I think his was the cheese before meat) I think I started to doubt my meat-first position. However, I had started with a position, and being a person of Rightness, I was stuck. I couldn't back down! (That wouldn't be Right.) So I had no choice except to fight for my Rightness. In the end, I lost. I missed out on eating pizza with my family, and I stubbornly refused my father's correction.

IS GOD A PRESBYTERIAN?

Although I'm certain God disapproves of daughters arguing with their fathers about cheese, I'm even more certain he particularly disapproves of his own children spewing their religious rightness all over the place. Jesus himself reserved his harshest criticism for the ones who thought they were so all-fired high and mighty and Right in the way they worshiped.

Ones like me.

Before I go on, I have to tell you that I have the best job anyone could have. As the religion reporter for a local daily newspaper over the past nine years, I've had the opportunity to listen to a wide cross section of Christian beliefs. I've heard it all. (Or at least a lot.) I've experienced nearly every style of Christian worship service and listened to a variety of theological explanations. I even know the difference between the Arminian and Reformed views of salvation. Unfortunately, as much as I love learning all about theology, it raises a question that continually haunts me: *Who is Right?* If we're all clinging to our various points of view as the Right way to do things, then it stands to reason that someone is wrong where they contradict.

I have a pastor-friend with whom I go round and round on this. One day I sat in his office and told him point-blank, "God's *not* Presbyterian, you know." As a Presbyterian pastor he laughed and said, "Of course he is!" But I don't think so. (Even though I'm Presbyterian too.) I don't think God's Catholic or Baptist or Pentecostal either. And I don't think he wants his people holing up behind their particulars, lobbing bombs at those who think differently. I think he'd like us to be more like pastor Randy Riggs.

I first met Randy several years ago. He's not like me, which in my book makes him Not Right. He's a Florida Cracker, a country preacher with a slow Southern drawl. At the time I met him he pastored a minuscule storefront church. No air conditioning. Out in the middle of nowhere. Metal folding chairs, an out-of-tune piano. He speaks in clichés and not in Proper Presbyterian English. For years he'd call me and tell me about his church, hoping I'd write a story in the paper. But...he just wasn't Right, you know?

Then one week my scheduled story fell through and I needed one ASAP. Just any old thing to fill the space. So remembering Randy Riggs, I gave him a call. Made it sound like I'd been wanting to do a story about him and his church all along. I met him at McDonald's, prepared to be silently, smugly Right, maybe even correct his simple, country-preacher ways. Show him the Right way. *My* way.

Then God had to go and ruin it all by showing me my Wrongness. As

Randy told me the story of his redemption and of the love he has for the lost of our community, I was stricken. There's no other word to describe it. Never before or since have I ever sat with a pastor who radiated the love of God as this man did. Here was a man, as opposite from me as they come, and I knew he was Right and I had been Wrong. About him, about whom God chooses to be his mouthpieces, probably about many things. What made it worse, Randy in all his Rightness was humbly oblivious to it. Even now, thinking about Randy brings a smile. He loves God and loves people. He even loves people like me who (Wrongly) snicker at poor storefront churches and country preachers.

So what does all this have to do with arguing over cheese on pizza, keeping score and having to win in relationships, and letting go of the idol of having to be Right? I think it has to do with fear and insecurity. When I'm afraid, I cling to whatever makes me feel important and safe. My opinions, my beliefs, my Rightness. As long as I'm Right, I'm okay. I have power. I call the shots. I keep the score.

But then God comes, drinking a cup of coffee in McDonald's, speaking slow and Southern-style. He lets you know that *he* knows what you think, but he loves you anyway and doesn't hold anything against you. He lets you know that because you belong to Christ he doesn't keep score.

When God comes and simply loves you in all your Wrongness, all your petty Rightness shrinks before your eyes and you realize how futile it all is. That there's only one Right way, the way of mercy and grace. That there's only one Right person, and it's not you. It's Jesus.

Then when you've been in his presence long enough and have experienced enough of his grace—his gift of favor and blessing when you deserve it least—you let go of the need to be Right. It's no longer important. What's important is going out and extending the mercy and grace you've been given to those you once thought were Wrong. Because now you know you're Wrong too. Wrong about pizza, wrong about people. Wrong…but forgiven.

Think on These Things

1. How addicted are you to being Right? Name some ways you either "keep score" or try to "win" in a relationship or insist on having the last word. What do you think would happen if you let things drop, if you were actually "wrong" (or not right)?

2. Where does this need to be right come from? (See James 4:1-3; Romans 7:15-20; Matthew 12:34.) What is the remedy? (See Romans 8:5-10; Galatians 5:4,6,13-16.)

3. Think about a situation or a relationship in which you have needed to be the "winner." How do the following passages from Ephesians 4 challenge and/or encourage you? How can you practically apply them to your life? Ephesians 4:1-6,20-25,29-32.

4. God does not keep score, and neither should we. However, we can't be merciful to others unless we realize how much mercy we've been shown. Meditate on the following scriptures, asking the Lord to open your heart to them:

Psalm 103:10-13

Daniel 9:9

Titus 3:4-7

---

*Let me tell something you need to remember. It's a sin to manipulate.
It's a sin to try to get people to be the way you want them to be by using low
blows, guilt-inducing comments and actions, and the rest of manipulation's
arsenal. It's a sin to say, "I'll stay here with the ironing and the washing
and the dirty diapers and the bottles while you go out to work every day
and have a nice lunch with all your friends."
…So how does one avoid manipulating or being manipulating?
The same way one can avoid any other sin:
by being set free from it through God's forgiveness and overcoming power.*
—Steve Brown, *Jumping Hurdles, Hitting Glitches,
Overcoming Setbacks*

Chapter 14

The Lone Rangerette Rides Again

Alone we can do so little; together we can do so much.—Helen Keller

You know how it is with toddlers. Wobbling around on their chubby legs, defiantly shouting, "I do it *myself!*" as they push or pull or try to lift some immovable object, while you, as the parent, chuckle to yourself and think, *No, Child. You can't do it yourself.* Then you watch in amusement until your precious cherub gives in to her frustration and either gives up or runs to you for help. You scoop her up in your arms, give her a hug and a box of apple juice, and either help her do what she wanted to do without anyone's help or put her down for a nap.

It's cute when a two-year-old tries to prove her self-sufficiency, but when those chubby legs have cellulite and belong to a middle-aged woman fighting a losing battle with a tree in her backyard…let's just say that *cute* isn't the word that comes to mind. There's nothing cute about a sweating, grunting, curse-hurling maniac of a woman in desperate need of either a shot of hormones or a reality check. Or a nap.

It had been building. *It* being my frustration and annoyance over the presence of a long-dead cypress tree in our backyard. It had been struck by lightning, and all that remained was a tall, brown skeleton. Every time I looked out my back window, all I could see was that ugly, dead tree. I wanted it removed, and I must have asked Barry a dozen times to take care of it. For some reason, he didn't consider it as high a priority as I did and put it way down on his to-do list—or the place on his list I call "the black hole."

Days, weeks, months went by, and the tree stayed put. Put and *dead*. Ugly, put, and dead. Finally I couldn't stand looking at it anymore and decided to do something about it *all by myself*. I wobbled on my chubby legs out to the backyard and pushed and pulled and yanked (and kicked and hit and yelled at) this immovable object.

Before you dismiss this as what my friend Cathy calls an NBD (No Big Deal), I must assure you it's a BD (Big Deal) because God used my fight with this dead tree and the resulting giant hole in my backyard to reveal one of the biggest idols in my life.

I, ME, MINE

I come by my self-reliance and Lone Rangerette spirit of independence honestly. My dad always taught me, "If you want something done right, do it yourself" and "The only person you can depend on is you." Couple that with my natural tendency toward being an introvert, a loner, and you have all the ingredients for a toddlerlike I-do-it-myself! mentality.

First of all, let me assure you (in case you happen to be a loner too) that being an independence-prone introvert isn't wrong or sinful in itself. It's just how God wired me (and perhaps you, too). Some people get their batteries recharged by being with people, while others require solitude to get rejuvenated. I don't know why that is, but it's on my list of things to ask God when I see him (right after I ask him about chin whiskers on older women and ear hair on older men).

The problems come when introverts start preferring the company of themselves to the company of others—when being with people is a nuisance and being alone is *divine*. (Leave it to a human to take something God created and turn it into an idol, which, as I've said before, is exactly what an idol is.)

As an introvert/loner, I enjoy being alone. For me, a good time is staying inside my house on my day off and only going out to get the mail. I don't chat on the phone (or even online); I don't do Tupperware parties or group lunches out. It drives my daughter Laura crazy because she's an extrovert with a telephone receiver glued to her ear. Torture to her is being home on a Saturday night with nothing to do and no one to talk to. My other daughter, Alison, is more like me. Ironically, she married an extreme extrovert who hates to be alone. (Pray for them!)

I married a loner like myself, which has its challenges too. Two do-it-yourselfers make for an interesting union. In our twenty-five years together, Barry and I have had a two-step dance going on. I take a step toward him; he steps back. He steps toward me; I run the other way. Not all the time, but often enough to get the message across: "I can do this marriage thing *all by myself.* You stay over there, I'll stay over here, and I'll let you know if and when I need you." It's not what God had in mind when he said, "The two shall become one flesh."

Part of my goal to be as independent (and nondependent on Barry) as I could be stemmed from wanting to know how to handle things if I were ever left alone (which is a good thing to learn). But as I've been telling you, an idol is a good thing elevated to a "highest" thing. In thinking about the need to do things on my own—check the oil in my car, know who to call when the toilet backs up—my highest goal became not needing Barry, or anyone else for that matter. *I don't need anyone! Just watch me—I can do it all by myself.*

Did you notice how subtly something good changes to something that enslaves? With my I'll-show-'em-all attitude, I became a fall waiting to happen. (As in, "Pride goeth before a fall.") That's how Lucifer fell from heaven and became the Enemy of our souls. That's how Adam and Eve fell when they desired to be like God.

So I went about my business doing things all by myself and taking great pleasure and pride in it too. I really didn't need anybody else! Anyway, dependence on others is for wimps. I may have even developed a swagger. *Hasta la vista, Baby. Go ahead, make my day. John Wayne, eat your cowboy/soldier heart out.* I couldn't see what was really going on: a deep and profound fear. A fear of being hurt, rejected, or disappointed if I let someone, even my husband, in too close. Better to keep everyone at arm's length. Best to put up a barrier. *You can get this close to me, but no closer. I set the terms; I draw the line. That way, I protect my own heart.* And that's the idol God showed me as I fought with the tree.

TREE V. ME

Although the cypress was twice my size, I knew I could take it. I could pull that baby up by its scrawny trunk and hurl it javelin-style across the back fence and into the woods. Then, once I hitched up my pants, scratched, and belched, I'd take on something else that needed taking on. Shingle the roof or dig a new well. After all, I could do it—all by myself. Just watch me.

Looking back on that day, I think I heard God laugh. I think he motioned to a host of angels and had them peer through the clouds just to watch me tangle with that tree. *Tangle*—that's a good word for it. Or maybe *tango.* You know, like that dance where one partner ends up bent over backward with thorns in her mouth. While I didn't have a rose between my teeth, I still ended up with a lipful of stickery prickles. That's what you get when you tango with a dead cypress tree.

I'd grab the trunk and pull one way until it catapulted back—*boing!*—the other direction. Then I'd hack at it for a while with a shovel and try digging up the root. That tree was as determined to stay put as I was to get rid of it. We squared off in a duel to the death, the tree egging me on, taunting me to give it my best shot. My hands were scratched and bloody, my feet were muddy from the mixture of dust and sweat inside my shoes. But I looked my foe in the limbs and said, "I can do this by myself."

I think that's when either God or the tree (or the voice of my imagination) replied, "No, Child. You *can't* do it yourself." But I was determined. I was *self*-reliant, *self*-dependent, *self*-sufficient. My dad's daughter. If I wanted something done right, then by golly I had to do it myself.

I tangoed with the tree all throughout the afternoon. By the time Barry was due home I had managed to dig it out, but not before knocking down part of the back fence, breaking the shovel, blistering both my hands, scratching myself from eyebrows to knees, and hurting my back. Plus, I left a hole in the yard big enough for me to fall into (and big enough for it to be a struggle climbing out). But as sore and achy as I was, I knew when Barry saw what I had done *all by myself,* he would fall down at my feet in awe and adoration. Maybe even take me out to dinner and buy me a diamond tiara. At least swear eternal devotion to me.

As I dragged the tree carcass—the spoils of my war—across the street to leave in the woods, I heard chuckling from heaven again.

Child, what are you doing?

"Who, me? I'm getting rid of this dead tree. All by myself. Did you see me, Lord?"

Yes, I saw you. Didn't you hear me laughing?

"I meant to ask you about that. What was so funny?"

It really wasn't funny, Child—you, struggling the way you do. Trying your hardest not to let anyone close. Hardening your heart to everyone around you. And for what? Blisters on your hands, a sore back, and a big hole in your backyard? What kind of victory is that?

"Gee, when you put it that way...But what about Barry? What about what he'll think when he gets home? He'll be proud of me!"

Will he? Or will he think you don't need him? How do you know that he won't be tempted to find someone who does? I didn't create you to do it alone, Child, and I'm not just talking about the tree. I'm talking about the way you keep to yourself. The brick wall you've erected that keeps people out. I created you incompletely, for loving dependence upon me. I like using other people to accomplish this. When you cut yourself off and refuse to let others in, you refuse me. You act like an orphan who thinks she has to shield herself and fight to survive, not like a daughter in a big, loving family.

"I'm sorry, Lord. I guess I forgot."

I guess you did. But that hole in your backyard will remind you. Child?

"Yes, Lord?"

Go wash up—you're a mess. But I love you.

"I don't deserve your love."

I never said you did. Now go hit the shower!

Now, don't think that I emerged from the shower suddenly ready to do the Tupperware party bit with all my neighbors. However, when Barry got home and I showed him the hole in the backyard and the blisters on my hands, I told him I should have waited for him and we could have done it together. He agreed, and then he laughed at my attempt to do it *all by myself.* Then I told him I needed him for other things too, not just tree-uprooting.

"He who separates himself seeks his own desire," wrote the writer of Proverbs. "He quarrels against all sound wisdom" (Proverbs 18:1, NASB). When I separate myself from others, I seek my own desire to be independent, an "island unto myself." Sound wisdom says the body of Christ works as a whole, the sum of its parts, with each part dependent on the others as it grows and builds itself up in love (Ephesians 4:16). Sound wisdom says, when I try to do things all by myself, I hurt not only myself (as evidenced by my tree-inflicted injuries), but the entire body of fellow believers whom God has placed around me to help me. For me to help. I hurt my family and friends by not allowing them in. I hurt God because by saying "I can do it myself," I spit in his face. There's no virtue in self-reliance, only rebellion.

"You're My Sister"

The tree episode opened my eyes, but Gerald and Amy, John and Billy Mack broke my heart. Gerald collects soda can pull-tabs and likes to count them. He wears a Hawaiian straw hat and likes to write down people's names. He's probably my age, although he'll never develop mentally past the age of ten.

Amy can't do much of anything, but she likes watching *The Price Is Right* and eating cookies. John is in a wheelchair and wants one of those fake frogs that "ribbits" when you walk past it. Billy Mack is just plain adorable. He doesn't talk much and doesn't have any teeth, but he smiles with his whole body.

I met these friends and two hundred or so just like them while working at a facility in our community that lovingly cares for mentally retarded and severely disabled adults. Although I worked there for only a short time, it was long enough to learn what it means to live interdependently within God's family.

My official position at the center was "substitute instructor's aide." As often as they needed me, I'd meet the bus, help those in wheelchairs maneuver through the halls, hold the hands of those who offered them to me, give and receive hugs, feed those who needed help, and basically do for those who could not do for themselves. Some of them could do nothing for themselves. They knew it and welcomed anyone and everyone. Even me. I took the job wanting to help, but I ended up being the one helped. From the first day when Gerald took my hand and introduced me around, gave me a big bear hug and said, "You're my sister," I knew I had fallen into something that wouldn't allow me to stay the same.

At lunchtime, I witnessed the more-abled wheel the less-abled to the lunchroom. The sighted brought lunch trays to the blind. Friends freely hugged and held hands—even men with men and women with women. When arguments erupted, others ran to comfort both the wronged and the instigator. They told each other as best they could, "It's okay. He didn't mean to hurt you. He can say, 'I'm sorry,' and you can say, 'Me too. I love you.'"

They told *me*, "I love you." Some drew me pictures. They all held my hands. And every day I'd go home and cry because I wanted to be like them.

One day we loaded up the buses and drove to the local high school football field for an athletic field day. We marched around the track and waved to the crowd in the bleachers. Then the athletes competed as best they could. I pushed Billy Mack in a wheelchair in the fifty-yard dash. (We lost, but he smiled anyway.)

Then four women ran a race. It took forever, especially since they all kept waiting for each other to catch up. They didn't realize they were competing against each other. As the crowd cheered, they cheered each other. Then, as they neared the finish line, they all linked arms and crossed it together.

And I came undone. It reminded me of what my pastor always says: "Brothers and sisters, none of us go to heaven alone. We go together—we go as a family."

I wanted so badly to be among those women on the track, linking arms with someone—being unafraid to link arms. But I have to be honest. I've held people off for so long, I'm not sure I know how to be any different. As I write this, I'm asking God to change me. But it's hard. This is one idol that's excruciating for me to let go of. I'm making progress though. Next month I'm going to a one-day women's conference with Cindi and some other friends. I recently joined a small group, too, where we study the Bible and pray *together*.

Like the racers in the track meet, I might take forever to get to the "finish line" of true interdependence, but I'll get there. I'll get there because God, our Father, has placed us with each other as a family—first to experience a loving dependence upon him, and then with each other. Linking arms, linking lives.

That way, when backyard trees need uprooting or races need to be run, we don't have to do it alone. Independently we get injured or left behind. Interdependently, we cross the finish line together, home free.

Think on These Things

1. Self-reliance is the American way of life, and we've grown up with this unbiblical notion of independence as a virtue. In what ways does society encourage a spirit of self-sufficiency? What keeps people from admitting their need of others?

2. In Revelation 3:14-21 Jesus speaks harshly to the church in Laodicea. What is his charge in verse 17?

3. Read Genesis 11:1-9. What were the people guilty of and what was God's response? What ways are Christians today guilty of the same things? (In what ways does this describe you?)

4. What do the following scriptures have in common with each other?
   John 13:34-35
   Hebrews 13:1
   Ecclesiastes 4:9-12
   Acts 2:42-47

5. Think about your own family, church, or community: What are some practical ways you can live out these scriptures? (For extra study: Using a concordance, look up all the "one another" scriptures in the Bible. What are we to do with and for one another?)

6. If we use the three *R*'s *(repent, replace,* and *rejoice)*, then we discover that freedom from self-reliance and rebellious independence comes only when we replace that need with God in order to rejoice. What do the following passages say about God? Take your time and dwell on them until you believe. Then *rejoice!*

Psalm 68:4-6

John 15:4-5

1 Corinthians 12:18,21-27

2 Corinthians 1:2-5

1 John 3:1

1 John 4:11

Blest be the tie that binds, our hearts in Christian love;
The fellowship of kindred minds, is like to that above.
—John Fawcett, "Blest Be the Tie That Binds"

Chapter 15

Fire Ant Fantasies

Always forgive your enemies. Nothing annoys them more.—Oscar Wilde

In Judith Viorst's book *I'll Fix Anthony*, Anthony's little brother is *ticked*. Although Anthony can read books, he won't read any to his little brother. He won't play checkers with him either. And even though the younger brother lets Anthony wear his Snoopy sweatshirt, Anthony won't let him borrow his sword.

"Mother says deep down in his heart Anthony loves me," says the little brother. But Anthony, "deep down in his heart," thinks his little brother stinks. So the little brother decides that when he's six, he'll "fix" Anthony. Then he describes what he'll do: When he's six and they both go swimming, Anthony will go *glug, glug* and sink. Only Anthony's brother will lose his teeth and get dimes from the tooth fairy, but Anthony's teeth will stay put no matter how much he wiggles them.

"When I'm six Anthony will still be falling off his bike," he says. "I'll ride by with no hands. 'Still falling off that bike?' I'll ask Anthony."[1]

I'll fix him. I'll get her. They'll be sorry.

Ah, revenge, as they say, is sweet. Just ask the woman whose husband just left her for another woman. As the story goes, she was walking the beach when she found a bottle in the sand. After pulling out the cork, a genie appeared and granted her three wishes. "Whatever you wish for," he said, "your husband will receive double of what you ask for."

The woman frowned, then smiled. "Okay, Genie. I wish for a million dollars."

Poof! A million dollars appeared at her feet and at the same time two million dollars appeared at the feet of her bum of a husband.

"Genie, for my second wish I'd like the world's most expensive diamond necklace."

Bingo! One for her, two for her creep of a mate.

The woman paused and asked the genie, "Is it really true that right now my lousy husband is enjoying two million dollars and more jewels than I do, and he gets double of whatever I ask for?"

"Those are the rules," he replied.

The woman thought long and hard, then smiled. "Okay, I'm ready for my last wish. I want you to scare me half to death."

She certainly fixed him! Now here's where I'm probably supposed to say, "Isn't that terrible of that woman to wish her husband dead?" But the truth is, if I were in that woman's place and had a genie at my disposal, I'd probably wish for the same thing. No, I'd wish for that adultering weasel to hover between life and death for three weeks while fire ants used his body as a target for biting practice. I'd wish for all his chest and leg hair to be hot-waxed and ripped off, and for ravens to peck out his eyes. Death would be too good for him!

Yes, revenge *is* sweet. Retribution is tasty. It's delicious when other people get their just deserts. (I'm sorry—I couldn't resist.) The trouble, is it's hard to find a genie in a bottle when you want to get even with someone. So you usually end up having to take care of it yourself.

TOO MUCH SWEETNESS

I don't remember her name. I just recall a scrawny blonde who stole my boyfriend in eighth grade. I loved him as much as a fourteen-year-old could after going steady for nearly a month. I think his name was Scott. (In 1969 most fourteen-year-old boys were named Scott, so it's a safe bet his was too.) *I loved him.* He played football and had silky blond hair. He let me wear his jacket and gave me his brother's class ring to wear (after all, this was only eighth grade).

I loved him. I wrapped pastel angora yarn around the ring to make it fit my finger. We passed notes in class and made out whenever and wherever we could. I gave him the best three weeks of my life.

Then *she* came along. (Actually, he had dumped me before he ever met her, but that's not how I like to remember it.) After all Scott and I had meant to each other, I knew I had to win him back.

So I killed her.

I trashed her reputation and spread vile lies about her. I was ruthless in my attempt to make her pay for what she had done to me. And I knew that as soon as Scott learned the truth about her, he would come running back to me.

I was right. He came running—and he brought his friends with him. They ambushed me on the football field and took turns telling me what a despicable creature I was and that I hadn't made What's-Her-Name look bad but had only exposed my own evil heart. Of course, they didn't say it quite that way, but instead used the language of angry eighth graders.

What I thought would be sweet revenge turned out to be a bitter poison. When you're in eighth grade and everybody hates you, you might as well crawl in a hole and die. My only saving grace was that it happened at the end of the school year and I only had to endure a few weeks of daggered stares and whispers behind my back until summer vacation.

It was sheer agony. Not so much the backlash against me, as painful as that was, but knowing I was capable of so much unbridled evil. I had always thought of myself as a good person. Ironically, I blamed the other girl for this revelation into my character and hated her even more. It was her fault that I reacted the way I did—she made me do it. If it weren't for her forcing me to do what I did, I could be Mrs. Silky Blond-Haired Scott right now.

The good news is that was over thirty years ago and I am older, wiser, more mature…and a Christian. All my thoughts of revenge have been nailed to the Cross, washed in the blood. And yet…while that's all true and I have been forgiven and have a new nature that desires to do right, I still like the thought of fire ants taking a bite out of someone I'm ticked at every now and then.

It seems like a lot of God's people feel the same way, at least many in the pages of the Bible did. Remember Jonah? He eventually escaped being digested fish food. The Bible says the Lord commanded the fish and it vomited Jonah onto dry land. (Heave-ho!) Then God told Jonah for a second time to go to Nineveh and tell them they were about to be toast. You can be sure Jonah obeyed the Lord this time. He preached to the Ninevites; they believed God and repented of their evil. When the Lord saw that, he had compassion on them and did not destroy them.

But instead of being happy for the Ninevites, Jonah got steamed. He ranted at God: *I told you this would happen! It's not fair. Those Ninevites are dogs and deserve to be wiped out.* After his tirade, Jonah found the best view on a hill outside the city, perhaps hoping God would change his mind again and rain a little hellfire and brimstone on the Ninevites. But God spared Nineveh, and the book ends with Jonah angry enough to die.

That's what the desire for revenge does to a person. While the Ninevites rejoiced in the grace and blessings of God, Jonah sat on a hill letting his own bitterness and anger eat him up.

THE BITE OF BITTERNESS

In *Reader's Digest,* E. Stanley Jones wrote, "A rattlesnake, if cornered, will sometimes become so angry it will bite itself. That is exactly what the harboring of hate and resentment against others is—a biting of oneself. We think we are harming others in holding these spites and hates, but the deeper harm is to ourselves."

I remember a particular crummy Mother's Day when I bit myself. Neither of my daughters was home that day. Alison had moved out of state with her army husband, Craig, and I'm not sure where Laura was. But that's not the crummy part. My husband was the crummy part.

Barry has always maintained that I am not his mother. While I don't dispute that, I do take issue with him not treating me like Queen of the World on Mother's Day. He usually gives me a card and buys me a cake, but he fails to understand that I deserve his servitude all afternoon. He only understands that on a Sunday afternoon in May, he wants to mow the lawn and work in the yard.

So that day I seethed. As I watched him from the dining room window, I dredged up every real and imaginable crime he had ever committed against me. He needed to be taught a lesson. He needed to pay for his sins against me. After much plotting (arsenic and old lace? a burning bed?), I decided the perfect revenge would be for me to run away.

I didn't go far, just to McDonald's. For about an hour I sat and nursed a cup of coffee along with my grudges. Then when I was certain Barry was sufficiently penitent, I drove home to enjoy the show. A bit of groveling, maybe a few tears. I imagined him panicked at my disappearance. Begging God for mercy upon his crummy soul. Vowing to be a Changed Person from Now On. I planned on withholding my forgiveness just long enough for him to earn it. Of course, I told myself that I wanted Barry to experience the "godly sorrow that leads to repentance" to bring him closer to Christ, but I really wanted him to be miserable and suffer because I was mad.

My heart beat in rapid anticipation as I practiced what I would say when I got home. *I wouldn't have had to run away and cause you such indescribable inner torment if you hadn't been such a jerk.* I had to keep pushing back annoying feelings of remorse on my part and mercy for Barry; they interfered with my revenge fantasy.

Unfortunately, I didn't have a chance to make my compelling speech. When I got home, Barry was still out in the yard. He hadn't even known I was gone! As far as he knew, I had been inside the house taking a Mother's Day nap or watching a movie. I couldn't believe it! What good is running away if the people you run from aren't weeping and wailing and gnashing their teeth because of your absence? What good is taking revenge if your victims don't suffer?

As for being bitten, my bitterness was minor and short-lived, but it bit me all the same. I had wished evil on my husband, even had hoped he'd fall into a patch of poison ivy or get cornered by a man-eating bunny rabbit.

I hope you're not too terribly shocked at my confession. Although I try to project an image of a cheerful, forgiving soul, sometimes the other me slips out. My evil twin thinks plotting revenge can be fun. It makes you feel all victim-y and put-upon, which in itself is enjoyable in a sick, twisted way. With revenge, after a while you can even convince yourself you deserve the pleasure of getting even with your enemies. As my friend Darby says, "There's nothing like a good smoting."

Except God says it's his job to smite people. Our job—of all things!—is to forgive them.

JUST AS IN CHRIST GOD FORGAVE YOU

Frankly, I like the idea of vengeance belonging to the Lord. After all, he can turn people into pillars of salt, change water into blood, and rain fire from heaven. He can confuse entire armies so they turn on themselves, cover the whole land with frogs, and flood the entire earth. On the other hand, at five feet two inches tall, what can I do that's even a fraction of what God can do? Give someone a piece of my mind? Wag my finger and look scary? Run away to McDonald's?

I say, let God do it. *I* say, just sit back smugly and wait for the plagues of locusts. However, *God* says, "Forgive your brother from your heart" (Matthew 18:35). He says to love your enemies, do good to those who hate you, bless those who curse you and pray for those who mistreat you (Luke 6:27-28). "If your enemy is hungry, bring her some lasagna; if she is thirsty, invite her over for tea. In doing this, you will heap burning coals on her head" (Romans 12:20, my paraphrase).

"Do not repay anyone evil for evil," Paul wrote to the church in Rome. "Do not take revenge, my friends, but leave room for God's wrath, for it is written: 'It is mine to avenge; I will repay,' says the Lord" (Romans 12:17,19). We have God's word on the matter—he will repay. He *will* repay. *He* will repay. He will right all wrongs, settle all scores, avenge all evil done against us. He has promised he will wipe away every tear (Revelation 21:4) and will set a table for us in the presence of our enemies (Psalm 23:5).

In the meantime, he tells us to forgive.

I hesitate to tell you all this because I haven't suffered any great wrongs in my life or had any deep pain inflicted on me. Maybe you have, and for me to say "Just forgive and go on" would seem cruel and insensitive. But because I care about you, I'd hate to see bitterness and unforgiveness eat you alive. I'd hate to see you continue in your sin. The Bible says to forgive "just as in Christ God forgave you" (Ephesians 4:32).

Yeah, but how many times do I have to forgive? Peter asked Jesus. *Seven?*

Peter, Peter, Peter, Jesus replied as he shook his head at his friend. *You think seven is being generous, but you're not even close. I want you to forgive long past the point where you think it's deserved. Forgive even when you think you can't. Forgive, forgive, and then forgive again—from the heart and not just lip service. Then Peter, I want you to forgive some more. Just as the Father has forgiven you* (from Matthew 18).

But I can't forgive So-and-So! You just don't understand!

Maybe I don't, but God does. And he *still* says, "Forgive, and then forgive again."

We can forgive because in Christ God has forgiven us. If we say we can't, it's not because we lack the resources (since all our resources belong to the Almighty), but because we ourselves are unrepentant of our own sin. Jesus said those who have been forgiven much love and forgive much. He ties our ability to forgive with our ability to repent.

If we hold grudges, it's because we have amnesia. We've forgotten how wretched we truly are. It's not just the prostitute who is wretched, but also the respectable Sunday school teacher who won't let go of a painful memory and the wish to pay back the one who caused it. Not just the drunken husband, but the wife who feels justified in withholding her affections as punishment.

If I cannot forgive, if all I can see is your sin against me, then I need to see how grievous my sin is against God and how much I need to be forgiven. I need to go back to the Cross and stay there until I know that I know that I know how costly forgiveness was and is.

CANCELED DEBTS

First of all, we are not performing some great act of benevolence by forgiving others. Forgiving is only doing our duty. God tells us to; therefore, it's required of us. However, we're not required to have warm, gushy feelings toward those we forgive. We don't have to *feel* forgiveness; we just have to do it.

Neither are we required to brush off the offense as insignificant. *Oh, it's okay that you set my hair on fire and shot my dog. Don't worry about it. I wanted to do something new with my hair, and the dog was old anyway.* On the contrary, forgiving someone means facing up to the debt that person owes us and then making the choice to forego further payment. It's like someone owing you a trillion dollars and you sending out a notice saying you've balanced the books and the person doesn't owe you a dime anymore. In business, once a debt is forgiven, a creditor cannot send a collection agency out after a debtor.

Forgiveness means no more

- cutting remarks or dirty looks
- dragging up the past
- demanding favors "because you owe me"
- self-righteous, phony niceness to make the other person feel miserable
- giving the cold shoulder
- gossiping
- seeking sympathy from others ("Can you believe what she did to me?!")
- rehashing scenes over in your mind to keep the anger fresh
- taking pleasure at the failure or pain of the person who hurt you
- fantasizing about fire ants.

Forgiveness also means

- praying for those who have offended you
- showing love in practical ways
- being as courteous and warm as possible
- seeking reconciliation when prudent
- admitting the truth about your part of the wrong (even if it's "only" holding on to bitterness).

Someone once said that when you refuse to forgive, you allow the other person to control you. That's true, but it's not why we should forgive. We forgive because God tells us to. We forgive because we have been forgiven much. If you have any doubts, just look at the Cross.

As Jesus died he prayed, "Father forgive them, for they know not what they do." He looked past our wickedness that put him there to our neediness. He did it to secure our forgiveness. He enables us to forgive others.

And when we do, he sets us free.

Think on These Things

1. Jesus once told a Pharisee, "He who has been forgiven little loves little." What do you think he meant by that? What does being forgiven have to do with loving others?

2. Read the parable of the unmerciful servant in Matthew 18:21-35. What does this passage say about you, your sin, and God's forgiveness? How have you acted like the first servant in the parable?

3. Read Ephesians 4:29–5:2. How would this passage help the first servant in the parable? (If you were to counsel him from this passage, what would you say?)

4. Jesus told the Pharisees and Sadducees to "produce fruit in keeping with repentance" (Matthew 3:8). In thinking about the subject of putting aside bitterness, forgiving others, and letting God take revenge, what kinds of fruit would repentance produce? (See Matthew 5:38-44; 7:1-5; and James 3:13-18.)

The gospel means that forgiveness is costly and requires death.
As you look at the parable (of the unmerciful servant in Matthew 18), who
took the debt? Who took the cost? Who paid the bill? When the king forgives the
debt, he is saying that he will pay it and take the loss. It is a form of death.
There is no forgiveness unless that is taking place. Unless you face the fact that
you are willing to take the loss, there is no forgiveness. My reaction is that I
will take the loss for five bucks, ten bucks, fifteen bucks; but at a certain point
I am not going to take the loss anymore. I don't have the resources within
myself. I am not a big-hearted king. Forgiveness means that I will really face
the debt and be willing to take the loss.
—Dave Desforge, World Harvest Mission "Sonship"
training program

Smile When Your Heart Is Aching

"It's snowing still," said Eeyore gloomily. "And freezing. However," he said, brightening up a little, "we haven't had an earthquake lately."
—Eeyore, *The House at Pooh Corner*

I'm not complaining, mind you, it being my Lot in Life and all. And while I prefer keeping my suffering to myself, it has occurred to me that by sharing my woe with you, you may be encouraged by my Bravery. Some may call me a martyr, others may call me a saint. Either way, because of my Great Difficulty in Life, I know a great reward awaits me in heaven.

It saddens me deeply to tell you this, but…I married a Sock Roller.

Although he's improved over the past twenty-five years, he still has this character flaw. He still takes off his dirty socks at the end of the day, rolls them up in sweaty little balls, and either throws them at me (usually aiming at my head) or, if I'm fortunate enough to be out of the room, he tucks them away in secret places for me to find weeks later.

I didn't know this about him before we got married, although there were clues. For example: the telltale lumps in his laundry bag in the corner of his air force barracks room. His roommate tried to warn me, but I simply ignored his pleas and even what I sensed in my gut. I'd seen one or two sock balls in the backseat of his car, but I turned a blind eye. Besides, I thought my love would change him once we were married.

I should have known better. My mother had always warned me against getting involved with a man who rolls socks. I can't be sure, but I suspect my dad had that same flaw when he was younger, although I never saw it. Maybe he was a closet roller—maybe he still is. Maybe I blocked it out of my memory. Maybe because of my father I was subconsciously drawn to Barry, destined to marry a Sock Roller in an effort to work out my suppressed feelings about my father.

I know what you're probably thinking. *Oh, you poor, poor woman. To have been burdened with this all these years and yet to have endured. Your example is truly inspiring. Of all women, you are most blessed. A true saint.*

If that's what you're thinking...you would be right, although modesty and humility prevent me from saying it myself. But you don't even know the half of it! Not only is my husband a sock roller, but he also thinks he's funny. When he's out in the yard working (and getting his socks as dirty and smelly as humanly possible), he'll wait until every pore in his body is at maximum sweat production, then he'll run into the house, find me, and either bury his head in my shirt (he prefers my white T-shirts) or hug me in such a way that my nose meets his armpits.

He thinks that's funny.

He thinks it's funny to sneak up behind me and yell "Boo!" just to watch me jump and hear me scream. He thinks it's funny to stuff his sneakers under the covers on my side of the bed or hide my pillow or wait until I'm snug and then untuck all the blankets. He thinks any joke that starts out "A guy walks into a bar" is hilarious. The man laughs so hard he cries when he watches the Three Stooges. At midnight.

But not only is he a Sock Roller who thinks he's funny, he also Cleans His Tools, Shines His Boots, and Oils His Mitt—*in the house.* Sometimes all at the same time in the same room. He'll get what he thinks is an old sheet or blanket, find the most inconvenient spot in the whole house, spread the sheet out and carefully place his items on it. Then after they've gathered dust for a week or two and I've tripped over them a dozen times, he'll clean/shine/oil them and let them sit for another few weeks. After all that he ends up with clean/shiny/well-oiled things and I have a sheet that I can cut up for rags.

But I'm not complaining. As I said, this is my Lot in Life. He's the husband God has given me. I've simply humbly, stoically accepted my marriage as my cross in life. Circumstances I must endure. *Grin and bear it.* Smile though my heart is aching. Keep a stiff upper lip and all that.

Sometimes it's hard. Sometimes I sit in church and watch the other women who are happily married to nonrollers, and I have to bite my lip to keep from crying (yet managing to sniff loudly so those around me will be Aware of My Suffering and ask if I'm all right). That gives me the opportunity to heave my shoulders and sigh. If the service hasn't already started or it's the stand-up-and-greet-someone part, I may offer a wan smile and shrug or nod. Even though I'm careful to only confide in a select three or four dozen close personal friends, people usually know just by looking at me that I'm married to a...*Sock Roller.* I'm known as "PoorNancyKennedy." *Poor Nancy Kennedy. She suffers well, doesn't she? Such an inspiration to us all.*

WHAT MISERY LOVES

You've heard it said that "Misery loves company," but that's not exactly true. What Misery loves is an audience. The more miserable I am, the greater my performance and the greater my need for an attentive audience. Without proper attention and recognition, my misery loses most of its twisted delight and sick pleasure. As a last resort I can take my pleasure in self-pity, but frankly, misery before an audience is so much more rewarding. Misery loves the spotlight. It's not enough to be on stage. To get full benefit, misery must be a solo act. With that in mind, here are the rules if you should ever meet me and I am experiencing a Time of Suffering because of my Lot in Life:

- If I am "sharing my story" (I *never* "complain"), you may not share your own story. Also, your story (which, again, you may not share) may never be more miserable or more pitiful than mine. There can be only one martyr at a time, and it is me. Author Louis Tartaglia illustrates this in his book *Flawless.* He writes about a minister whose wife constantly cheated on him with younger men. Everyone knew it, yet the minister refused to do anything about it. Instead, he vowed to show his congregation that prayer and patience could change anyone. However, in therapy he admitted he didn't want her to change. "He loved the idea that he was a martyr at the matrimonial altar," he writes. "He prided himself on being the perfect victim. It liberated him to admonish all those who didn't suffer as well as he did." This brings me to my next rule:

- You must never offer solutions to my woe, only sympathy. Acceptable expressions include "You've endured so much," "How do you cope?" and "I could never do what you do." You're encouraged to ask for my advice for a similar situation, but without actually talking about your problems. Remember: The focus must always be on me. Since I am Most Miserable, my advice is gospel. (Not *the* gospel, of course, for that would point out my sin and the idol of my self-pity. However, you are free to be convicted of your own sin and repent at any time.)

- You must also never—and I can't stress this rule enough—suggest that I am to blame for my own misery. It is never my fault. It is always someone else's. Others are bad; I am good. I am Long-suffering and Patient, storing up treasures in heaven. Earning points with God and all the angels. Maybe even earning the biggest mansion in heaven. After all I've suffered, Lord knows I certainly deserve it....

WHAT MISERY HATES

Misery loves illusion and fantasy, but it hates truth. The miserable one imagines himself or herself exalted and special. The greater the suffering, the greater the honor. Misery especially loves using guilt to get "deserved" honor and attention. Mothers especially love using guilt:

- "I don't mind. My fever's only 105 degrees, and the doctor says I shouldn't go out, but if you have to meet your friends at Taco Bell, even though it's raining (cough, cough), I don't mind driving you."

- "Don't worry about missing my birthday. I'm only your mother who carried you for ten months and was in labor for fifty-seven hours until they had to call in a specialist who did a C-section without anesthesia because I didn't want my precious baby to suffer any unnecessary trauma."

- "Of course you can move out. It's okay that I just spent the last month redecorating your room just the way you like it."

- "The only crime I'm guilty of is loving you."

Misery and self-pity thrive on the idea of being singled out for attention. Misery demands special treatment. ("Be nice to me, for I've already Suffered Much.") It loves manipulation of others. But it hates truth.

When someone is held by misery and self-pity, others often see it as a virtue. We admire someone who holds up well despite intolerable circumstances or shows grace in adversity. That's what we see on the outside. But for those who are clinging to this worthless idol of self-pity, what we don't see is their hearts. Here are some questions you might ask yourself when you find yourself down in the doldrums:

- How do I respond when someone asks about my situation? Do I become animated and energized when retelling my story? Or the opposite, morose and melancholy? Do I whine? Complain? Assign blame to another person?

- What do I hope to accomplish by telling (and retelling) my story? How many people have I told? Do I make sure to name names? Am I trying to get people on "my side"?

- What do I do with advice I'm offered? Do I counter every suggestion with "Yeah, but…"?

- Do I really want this situation to change?

WWJD?

In the gospel of John, Jesus went up to Jerusalem and stopped at a pool called Bethesda where a great number of disabled people lay around near the water. As was believed, from time to time an angel of the Lord came down and stirred up the water. When that happened, the first one into the water was cured.

Among the people was a man who had been an invalid for thirty-eight years. Jesus approached him and asked, "Do you want to get well?"

What an odd question. But Jesus knew the man's heart. He knew how he had spent the past thirty-eight years swapping stories with his fellow invalids about HMO red tape and the high cost of prescription drugs. He knew about the hierarchy—from Most Miserable to Least Miserable—and whose Lot in Life was the worst. He knew that to be well meant changing one's whole identity. No longer known as "that poor man who cannot walk" but as just another healthy Joe who no longer would have an excuse not to get a job.

Do you want to get well?

"Sir," the invalid replied, "I have no one to help me into the pool when the water is stirred. While I am trying to get in, someone else goes down ahead of me."

Just imagine: He had played the role of the invalid for nearly four decades and probably couldn't imagine any other life. Instead of answering, "Yes, Lord! I do want to get well," he gave his standard, whiny response. (My husband would say of that man, "He'd complain if he was getting hanged with a new rope.")

But Jesus knew what he had come to do, so he told the man, "Pick up your mat and walk." Then Jesus slipped away, but later he found the man and said, "See, you are well again. Stop sinning or something worse may happen to you" (John 5:6-14).

When we're held by misery, Jesus comes and asks, "Do you want to get well?" Do you want to step down from your starring role as Martyr, put away the chips and dip from your pity party, and start a new life with a new identity?

He offers us wellness and wholeness, freedom from the need to be pitied. He asks, "Do you want it?" If we do, Jesus says, "Then get up!"

Whatever idol holds us, God requires that we make a move. Just as the Old Testament King Jehoshaphat removed the Asherah poles (used in idol worship to the goddess Asherah) from Judah, we have to take a step to remove our idols. They don't get up and move on their own. On the contrary, by our doing nothing, they only hold on to us even tighter.

With the idol of misery and self-pity, the first step is to repent. (Of course.) But as part of repentance comes a getting up or a walking away. It's looking at Misery and unmasking the lie it promises. Misery says, "You're only special because of your miserable circumstances, not because of who you are. Being a victim gives you moral superiority. Without your misery, you're nothing."

Once the lie is unmasked, we can walk away from it. We can say, "I believed it in the past and it held me captive. But now that I see it for what it really is, Misery has no more power over me. *It's just a lie.* My circumstances don't give me meaning and identity, only my life in Christ does."

Does this mean if I repent of my idol of misery and self-pity my husband will stop rolling his dirty socks and throwing them at me? Probably not, although miracles do happen. More likely it means the more I see my self-pity as sin equal to his sock rolling, the easier it will be to stop feeling morally superior. It levels the playing field—we're both sinners in need of grace.

After he healed the invalid, Jesus slipped away into the crowd, but later he sought the man out. He went to him. Jesus comes to us in our circumstances too.

Pretend you're married to a Sock Roller (or a harsh or lazy man, an alcoholic, an unbeliever. Or maybe a basically terrific guy who works long hours or hates your cat). *Something* that irritates you or causes you constant grief. Your challenge is to go from misery to freedom without jumping ship. The question is, how are you going to do it?

Here's what I suggest:

- Begin by seeing your life (and the people in it) as an adventure or a challenge, not a burden. Ask God to give you new eyes and a new perspective: What good things have I missed by concentrating on the bad?

- Next, look for evidences of God visiting or coming to you. How is he answering your prayers concerning your situation? Are your circumstances changing, or is your attitude different? If you're the one changing, how are people around you responding to the changes in you?

- Expect God to do good things in your life.

A troubled father once came to Jesus and begged him to help his boy who was possessed by an evil spirit. He told Jesus, "'If you can do anything, take pity on us and help us.'

"'"If you can"?' said Jesus. 'Everything is possible for him who believes.'

"Immediately the boy's father exclaimed, 'I do believe; help me overcome my unbelief!'" (Mark 9:20-24). This man doubted Jesus' ability. I don't ever doubt whether God *can* do something. I'm just not always sure that he *will*. So I just assume he won't. (Isn't that sad? Especially if you're God.)

But just as Jesus went to the man he healed and had compassion on the doubting father, he comes to me with compassion. He leaves me in my circumstances but changes my heart toward those around me. When I ask him to reveal himself to me, to give me a glimpse of hope, he does. He brings a word, a phrase, a verse from a song, a passage in a book, a scripture that changes me from the inside out.

Whenever my face is dragging in the dirt and I'm thinking like Winnie the Pooh's gray donkey friend, when I'm consumed with circumstances and losing hope, God comes to me. Whether it's through a radio program, in a sermon, a book, or an e-mail from a friend, he stoops to remind me that he is able to do immeasurably more than all I ask or imagine, according to his power that is at work within me (Ephesians 3:20). It's always that same message, and it always bolsters my pessimistic heart.

Then before I know it, my self-pity is replaced with hope. With the God of hope himself.

Think on These Things

1. What kinds of situations cause you to fall into self-pity? What are some of your most pitiful thoughts?

2. Every idol promises a benefit. What is the "benefit" from self-pity? What are some circumstances that result in self-pity? Some examples in Scripture include:

Genesis 4:4-8

1 Samuel 1:4-8

Proverbs 13:12

Colossians 3:12

3. The antidote to self-pity is hope. Take the following scriptures and write a sentence or two about how they can be applied to your current situation. (Bonus: Memorize one or more of them to help keep you pity-free.)

Psalm 40:1-3

Psalm 42:5

Psalm 46:1-3

Psalm 71:5

Isaiah 40:31

Jeremiah 29:11

Romans 5:1-5

Romans 12:12

4. Read Romans 15:13. Make this your personal prayer, asking the God of hope to come to you and be your encouragement.

———————

There are no hopeless situations;
there are only people who have grown hopeless about them.
—Clare Boothe Luce

Chapter 17

Move Over, Victoria—I Know the Real Secret!

Prayer and sex are words seldom used in the same sentence.
But they should be.—Kathy Peel

He wasn't supposed to laugh. I had imagined a dozen reactions, but laughing definitely wasn't one of them. This happened in the early days of our marriage when I was Young and Restless and eager for romance. I'd gotten my hands on a book that told all the how-to's of putting a smile on a husband's face. It promised that if I'd do this one thing, I could guarantee my sweetie would be smiling for a week.

So I tried it. Wrapped myself in plastic wrap. Naked.

When my unsuspecting husband came in from his Saturday softball game and beheld me in all my Saran-wrapped glory, he smiled all right. Then he laughed. Threw back his head and roared. Called me a nut. Couldn't get over what a joker I was. *Asked about leftovers from the previous night's meat loaf in the fridge.* Laughed some more. Then, not realizing that my intent was *not* to be laughed at, but an attempt at wooing him with my charms, he turned on the television and flopped on the couch. Meanwhile, I peeled myself in the bathroom and cried.

Not one to give up easily, a week or so later I drove eighty miles to the nearest Victoria's Secret to discover what her "secret" was. From what I could tell, it involved a lot of sheer fabric and strategic padding. So with single-minded purpose (to get my husband's blood boiling and win his undying love and devotion forever), I carefully chose a pale pink satin nightie with spaghetti straps.

All the way home I planned my move. I'd wait until Barry locked the front door for the night, then I'd disappear into the bathroom to change and make my grand entrance.

At just the right moment, I slunk into the bedroom, a seductive tigress in pink. He didn't laugh this time. Instead, he smiled an odd half-smile, then went into the kitchen for a drink of orange juice. As he chugged, any thought of romance I may have had earlier immediately grew icicles. You could have kept a side of beef fresh for a month in that bedroom, if you know what I mean. *After I drove 160 miles to get this stupid nightgown…it'll be a cold day in a hot place if he thinks I'll warm up to him any time soon.*

It turned out my husband has an aversion to slick fabric. He's afraid his rough, mechanic's hands will snag it. But he didn't tell me then. He was afraid to hurt my feelings, I later found out. That night he just quietly crawled into bed after finishing his orange juice, kissed me good night on the cheek, and kept his distance while I stared into the darkness, not understanding what was going on. Not understanding much of anything, least of all the whole concept of holy and pure sexual expression and sacred romance in marriage. I only knew what I had seen in the movies and on soap operas. I didn't know about selfless love and unashamed nakedness. Twenty-five years later, I think I'm finally starting to get it.

LOOKING FOR LOVE IN ALL THE WRONG PLACES

I've been thinking a lot about what I want to tell you and how I should say it. Sex is such a touchy subject. It touches the core of who we are. For some, just the word brings tears. For others, giggles. My feelings about it lie somewhere in between. Anyway, here are my options: I could tell a couple of funny stories of failed attempts at romance, maybe about the frustrations of being interrupted by kids who can't sleep or about the whole Men-Are-from-Mars/Women-Make-a-Big-Deal-Over-Candles-and-Sweet-Talk thing, then tack a spiritual message on the end. Or I could dance around the subject, merely hinting at what I really want to say and hope that you can decipher my message among clever words. Or I could pour out my heart to you about what I think and feel and have come to know about sex, love, and romance, in the hope that by doing so, God will set us both free. I think I'll try that option.

Whenever I give my testimony, I often begin by saying, "If my life were a song, it would be 'Looking for Love in All the Wrong Places.'" Then I add, "I was boy crazy from birth." It generally gets a laugh, and people get the idea without my having to spell it out. What I don't tell them is the details. I don't think I need to tell them to you either. I have a hunch you may have "details" in your life as well, or at least you may know someone who has. I will tell you that the worst piece of advice I ever received came from a classmate of mine in junior high school. I had just been dumped by the Blond-Haired Scott that I told you about earlier, and his friend clued me in on the secret to a man's heart. He used crude words—and he was wrong—but I believed him and followed his advice for the next six years, offering myself to anyone who would tell me he loved me, and hurting so badly because of it that I cried almost every day.

Then I met Barry. He invited me ice skating and bought me a pair of skates because the rental shop didn't have any in my size. No man had ever bought me anything of any value before, so I asked him to marry me. Since no woman had ever proposed to him before, he said yes. Three months later we got married.

To be honest with you, sex and those size-seven ice skates were the only things Barry and I had in common. And once the ice melted and I put the skates away, sex was all I had left to connect me with my husband. I held on to that bad piece of advice from junior high school and made it my goal to do all I could to gain Barry's "love."

That's all I ever wanted—someone to love me. Someone to cherish me. To rejoice over me and love me enough to die for me. I just never knew I could be loved without having to give my body in return. Even in marriage, where sex is supposed to be an expression of commitment and unity, a joining of hearts as well as bodies, I still felt it was a commodity. A product, a service. My thinking had been warped by my own past sin and confusion, and I was racked with guilt. Naked and ashamed.

Although I enjoyed sex, and Barry was and still is a great guy, I desired more from him. I wanted romance, especially the soap opera variety. Mood lighting and candles. Poetry and music. Perfectly choreographed, no distractions, and with champagne and caviar. Or at least ginger ale and cheese. The only problem was, I married a Gatorade-and-fish-sticks kind of guy who'd rather I wear an old hockey jersey than satin and lace. Even when I'd try my hardest to create the perfect mood, much like a director sets the stage for a play, my costar had his own ideas. To his credit, Barry only wanted me for me; I wanted him to give me more than he was able. Physically, I couldn't ask for more. It was the ache inside that I wanted him to kiss away.

So what do you do when you have all these conflicting emotions: a need to be loved, a guilt from the past, a desire for intimacy, a fear of rejection, an unmet longing that you try to fill the only way you know how that just remains unfilled? What do you do when all you want is attention, all you want is to have romance and to feel loved? What you do is try harder. You read more books and attend more seminars. You plan romantic getaways and redecorate your bedroom. You read romance novels and listen to love songs and try to imagine they're about you. Feeling worse, you pine for the hole in your heart to be filled and you try even harder. In doing so, you set yourself up for disappointment—or worse. When you get tired of struggling to get your needs met at home, without meaning to, you take your vulnerability elsewhere and end up in situations that only compound and complicate the pain you felt in the first place.

At first he's just someone you work with, or the guy who mows the neighbor's yard, or your son's best friend's newly divorced dad who asks for your advice at a soccer game. He might not even be particularly handsome, but he pays attention to you. He laughs at your jokes and appears interested in what you have to say. You know you would never cheat on your husband, but…before you know what hit you, you find yourself preoccupied with thoughts of seeing him again, dressing so he'll notice, thinking of the private jokes between you. Pretty soon you find yourself fantasizing about what his arms would feel like holding you or what his kisses would be like. In an instant, you discover you've crossed the line between innocent friendship and immorality. Even if nothing physical ever takes place, you know it's wrong.

And you're trapped. Ironically, what motivated you in the first place—the desire for intimacy—ends up being the very factor that keeps you from getting what you so desperately want. You believe the lie that promises intimate fulfillment, but what you end up with is more guilt, more shame, more frustration, and unfulfilled desires. And you're angry—at yourself, at your husband, at God who refuses to answer your prayers in the first place (or so you think).

THE GREAT PURSUIT

When I tell my story and talk about being "boy crazy from birth" and how I proposed to my husband, I say, "Even after we got married, I continued looking for love. Then three years into our marriage, I met someone who loved me the way I always knew love should be. Then *I* received a marriage proposal. Almighty God called my name from heaven and said, 'I have loved you with an everlasting love; I have drawn you with loving-kindness' (Jeremiah 31:3). He said, 'Seek [my] face,' and I answered him, 'Your face, LORD, I will seek' (Psalm 27:8)."

I wish I could say that ever since then I stopped chasing elusive, romantic dreams—but I didn't. After all, I learned early on to be a pursuer. Even with my own husband. If I hadn't proposed to him, I don't know if I still might be single or not. As it is, I don't know what it's like to have a man, sweaty palms and cracking voice, nervously ask for the honor of my hand in marriage. It's part of the consequences I bear from chasing after my idol.

But God. My two favorite words! But God pursued me, as a Bridegroom pursues the woman of his desire. "Say to the Daughter of Zion," wrote the prophet Isaiah, 'See, your Savior comes! See, his reward is with him, and his recompense accompanies him.'…you will be called *Sought After*" (Isaiah 62:11-12, italics mine).

The everlasting love of the Savior, drawing me, his beloved, with loving-kindness, is what I long for most. That's the real thing. On the other hand, sex between a husband and his wife is a picture of that deep love. Ideally, it's the closest thing on earth to God's love: vast, unmeasured, boundless, free.

I have to confess, after more than twenty years of reading the Bible I still don't fully comprehend God's intentions for sex within a marriage, although I'm beginning to grasp it. When married sex and romance is good, it's glorious. It's soul-connection. It's comfort in life's crises and communication when words won't suffice. It's being naked and unashamed before God, and knowing that he approves. That he enters into the bedroom with the two of you and whispers, *It is good. It is* very *good.* And you know it, deep in the core of your being.

SINGLE SEXUALITY

While God created us as sexual beings, not all of us have the God-sanctioned opportunity to express our sexual desires. I don't even pretend to understand it; I only know what is. Even as a married person I have, at times, used sex as an idol—or as a means to a greater idol, which is human love and acceptance. But as I continue learning to find my fulfillment in the love of God, sexual expression becomes less of a selfish act, and more of a self-less one. A giving of myself, rather than a taking for the sole purpose of my own pleasure.

My friend, if you are single, either through divorce, death of your spouse, or because you've never married, know this: Your ultimate fulfillment is found in Christ. Listen to what the psalmist wrote:

> O God, you are my God, earnestly I seek you; my soul thirsts for
> you, my body longs for you, in a dry and weary land where there is
> no water.... Because your love is better than life, my lips will glorify
> you.... On my bed I remember you; I think of you through the
> watches of the night. Because you are my help, I sing in the shadow
> of your wings. My soul clings to you; your right hand upholds me.
> (Psalm 63:1-8)

Author Rosalind Rinker writes in the *Women's Devotional Bible*, "We thirst for different things at different times: recognition, friends, a life-mate, a home, children...But most of all we thirst to love and be loved." We thirst for romance and for sexual fulfillment, but ultimately, our thirst is for God. *He* is the one we long for. *He* is the one whose love is better than life. *He* is enough. If he weren't enough, he wouldn't be God. Since he's God, he is enough to meet all our deepest longings.

Just last week I got a call from a single friend. A year ago, I had watched her struggle—and fall—in this delicate area of sexuality. Although she wanted desperately to be strong in her Christian commitment, she was lonely. She longed to be held by a man. And she fell into sin. I remember her anguish and her guilt, her anger and her shame. It was only one time, but it was one time too many, and she knew it.

When she called last week, she had good news. She said that she is finally discovering contentment in her singleness, in all areas of her life. She said God was and is enough for her.

My friend, he promises to be enough when you're single, and enough when you're not. He's enough when you're married to a man who fails to physically or emotionally satisfy you. He passionately pursues his beloved and quenches her deepest thirst.

As for the *real* secret of sexual fulfillment? Move over, Victoria—it's Jesus, the one true Lover of our souls.

Think on These Things

1. Sex and romance are used to sell everything from toothpaste to automobiles. What are some of the common lies and myths about sexuality that abound in society today?

2. According to the following Scripture passages, what is God's purpose for sex in marriage?

   Genesis 1:28

   Genesis 2:18,24-25

Genesis 24:67; 2 Samuel 12:24

Deuteronomy 24:5

Song of Solomon 4:10

1 Corinthians 7:3-5

3. Growing up, what were some of the messages you learned about sex? How do they align with the Word of God?

4. What are some of the consequences (spiritual, physical, and emotional) of sex outside of marriage? (See Ephesians 5:5 and Colossians 3:5-6.) With the help of a concordance, list some of the verses that talk about sexual sin. Why do you think God places so much emphasis on it? What is the hunger that drives sexual obsession?

5. Read Psalm 63. In the area of your sexuality, choose one or more of the verses of this psalm and turn it into a prayer to the Lord. (Bonus: Write your prayer down and refer to it often.)

In the midst of the pleasure and beauty found in sexual intimacy is always the duty to follow the designer's plan for reciprocity as each partner seeks to meet the needs of the other and for exclusivity as each protects the treasured "one flesh" relationship. This intimacy may then be fully enjoyed and the purpose of the Creator fulfilled. We dare not prostitute through our own selfishness and unbridled desires the unique intimacy that is God's glorious seal of unity on the marriage.

—Dorothy Patterson, *Women's Devotional Bible*

Chapter 18

Too Good to Be True

If you wish to be good, first believe that you are bad.—Greek proverb

When my sister was about seven or eight, she wiped spaghetti sauce from her mouth with a piece of bread. This is a significant event in our family's history because, as the Good Daughter, it is the one and only time Peggy ever got in trouble.

It happened in a nanosecond. As we all sat around the dinner table taking turns reporting what we learned in school that day, Peggy did the bread-wipe and Dad reached across my place at the table and whacked Peggy's hand. We were all stunned. Not that Dad had whacked one of us, but that it was Peggy. *How could this be? Not Peggy—she's the Good Daughter!*

It turned out not to be a willful act of rebellion or even playful mischief. Peggy had watched Dad sop up spaghetti sauce on his plate with a piece of bread, and to her child-logic, sauce was sauce, whether on a plate or a face. She was only doing what Dad did, or so she thought. We all felt terrible. Dad felt awful for thinking his little Peggy could do anything bad. Not Peggy!

Shortly after that, Dad bought Peggy a hamster named Daisy. Since he had never bought me a hamster, I considered wiping my face with bread too, in hopes that I could get a present, but I thought better of it. I had received my share of much-deserved whacks over the years and wisely discerned that I probably wouldn't get away with it. I had a feeling only Good Daughters got hamsters after they got in trouble.

ROCK STACKERS, HUT BUILDERS, AND FINGER POINTERS

In his book *In the Grip of Grace,* Max Lucado tells a parable of five sons.[1] The eldest was the obedient son (a picture of Jesus), the other four were rebellious (that's you and me). I won't go into the whole story because the entire book is so great that you should read it for yourself. But I do want to tell you about three of the rebellious sons.

One son Lucado called a Rock Stacker. (A "Good Daughter," you could say.) After being separated from his father, his mission in life was to build a pathway across a raging river by stacking rocks, with each rock representing a good deed. This son worked hard, carefully doing everything right, faithfully spending a minimum of a half-hour in daily quiet time "doing devotions" and praying for the sick and needy. He also regularly collected cans of tuna and boxes of corn muffin mix for the hungry, visited men in prison, and shared the Four Spiritual Laws with people he met in the market checkout line. He was the son who studied the Ten Commandments, the Beatitudes, 1 Corinthians 13, and the book of James, trying with all his might to do everything that was written down in the Scriptures. He even added a few dozen regulations of his own. He never missed a Sunday worship service or a Wednesday prayer meeting. He volunteered in the nursery, loved his wife, was kind to his children, and kept his radio tuned only to Christian stations.

Although he was stressed out most of the time, he was always looking for something more he could do: a list he could check off, a formula he could follow. He was a son, but he didn't feel son-ish. He felt slave-ish and unsure. So he worked as hard as he could in a futile attempt to reach his father on his own, refusing his eldest brother's offer of carrying him across the river. He believed since he had gotten himself separated from his father, it was up to him to find a way back. "Rock upon rock, I will stack until I have enough rocks to travel upstream to [my father's] castle. When he sees how hard I have worked and how diligent I have been, he will have no choice but to open the door and let me into his house."

Another of the sons Lucado calls a Hut Builder. Hut Builders are not Good Daughters. They go without calling their mothers for months at a time and watch Ricki Lake in the afternoon when they know it will only further corrupt them. They live for their own comfort and pleasure. They're lenient parents because they can't tolerate the turmoil and commotion involved in setting down and enforcing family rules. Hut Builders like to go to church because it makes them feel good (their motto being, "If it feels good, do it"). They like seeing their friends and being seen by others. During the fellowship hour they rush to the coffee and doughnuts (while the Rock Stackers rush to the kitchen to see what they can do to help). They like the idea of grace and freedom in Christ because they secretly think that means they can get away with slacking off. They pray because they want the answers. They study their Bible because they like learning and gathering knowledge. As for obedience, Hut Builders would rather not think about it—ruins their mood.

The Hut Building son forgets about the joy and pleasure of living in his father's presence and instead builds his hut out of straw and twigs and makes his home in the world, living only for the moment at hand.

The third son was a Finger Pointer. He kept himself busy by comparing himself to his other brothers and concentrating on their sins rather than his own. If someone pointed out his faults he would stiffen his back and reply, "That may be so, but at least I don't _____." Then he would proceed to describe in great detail the goings-on inside the Hut Builder's shack, or even the inconsistencies in the Rock Stacker's life. Finger Pointers do just that. They point at others in an effort to divert attention from themselves. Or they do so to attract attention *to* themselves as if to say, "Next to So-and-So, I look pretty good." Finger Pointers are self-appointed critics, believing it's their Christian duty to critique the pastor's sermon or broadcast to the congregation just what they think they saw the pastor's wife buying at the liquor store.

Outwardly, Finger Pointers act as if they were immaculately conceived, but deep inside they're afraid their own illegitimacy will be revealed. "As long as I can be better than my neighbor," a Finger Pointer says, "then maybe God won't notice my failures." Finger Pointers are bitter and insecure, hating both the sin *and* the sinner. The Finger Pointing son forgets that he is part of the "all" in "All have sinned and fall short of the glory of God" in Romans 3:23. He forgets that he is just as separated from the father by the river as his brothers are, and that only the obedient eldest brother can bring him back.

Did you see yourself in any of the sons? I hate to admit it, but I think I'm all three of them rolled into one. "Quite a trio, don't you think?" Lucado writes of them. "Though they may appear different, they are very much alike. All are separated from the Father. And none is asking for help. [One] indulges his passions, [one] monitors his neighbors, and [one] measures his merits. Self-satisfaction. Self-justification. Self-salvation. The operative word is *self.* Self-sufficient. 'They never give God the time of day' (Romans 3:18, MSG)."

FALLING INTO "PENANCE MODE"

Although I'm predominantly a Hut Builder, I do have Rock Stacking tendencies, especially when it comes to how I handle my guilt feelings. I call it falling into "penance mode." It goes something like this: Either I have a flashback of some past sin or else I'm in the middle of a current sin and want to repent. Now, I wholeheartedly believe that 1 John 1:9 is true: If I confess my sin, God will forgive me and purify me. I believe it in theory. But inwardly, I still want to *do* something. I want to help God out in this process of forgiveness.

Generally my guilt feelings don't motivate me toward doing good deeds in order to atone for my sin (after all, I'm a Hut Builder). I'm more prone to trying to feel as guilty as I can for as long as I can. I grovel; I mope. I replay every word, every action, every thought and nuance of my sin. I call all my friends and tell them what a pathetic excuse for a human being I am and that they really could do better than to have me as a friend. Then I either avoid God's voice telling me to "Come now, let us reason together.... Though your sins are like scarlet, they shall be as white as snow" (Isaiah 1:18) and his promise that "as far as the east is from the west, so far has he removed our transgressions from us" (Psalm 103:12), or I repeatedly howl for mercy and forgiveness (which he's already given me). At least ten times for little sins, indefinitely for the biggies.

Also when I'm in penance mode I'm careful to not accept any type of ministry invitations—giving a testimony at church, writing an article, speaking at a retreat. *I'm not worthy enough,* I tell myself. *I'm too sinful. I still haven't logged in enough extra Bible reading and prayer time. Besides, I left a shopping cart in the store parking lot on purpose and lied to a neighbor, which only proves I'm too far gone to minister to anyone else. I'm slime. I'm bug slime. I'm squished-bug-on-a-windshield slime. I use the word "darn" and don't even think it's bad that I do.*

The last time I was in penance mode my daughter Laura nailed me. She told me, "Mom, whenever you do something wrong you walk around all depressed, feeling sorry for yourself, like your sin is too bad for God to forgive. Get over it. You say you're a Christian, well then act like one!"

I'm still mulling that one over. I mean, that's the gospel, pure and simple. We sin, our Father forgives. We walk in forgiveness, cleansed and renewed. Still...it doesn't *feel* like enough. There's got to be more I can *do.* Something *I* can do. Five easy steps, four secrets, twelve tips, ten or eleven commandments I can keep. It's not right that I need God to do for me what I can't do for myself. He's such a busy God, and I'm quite capable. *Just let me help!*

But there's nothing I can do to help because Christ has done it all. Jim, a pastor-friend of mine, gave me this advice recently: "Take one look at your sin and ten looks at Christ." He added, "We do need to acknowledge the seriousness of our sin and not pass it off flippantly as some people do by offering a haphazard 'I'm sorry' when they might not even be sorry. On the other hand, some people take ten looks at their sin and that's what they dwell on instead of how good it is to be forgiven."

What we need, then, is a contrite celebration. A humble rejoicing in the mercy of God. Although when I'm in penance mode I *feel* humble, what I really am is proud. My pride reveals my idol, which is my own self-righteousness. All my guilt feelings, my thoughts, all my wanting to do something to help get rid of my sin and put me back in right-standing with God all point to the fact that I'm trusting in my*self*, not in my Father, for redemption.

It always comes back to self. I'm my biggest obstacle. My number one problem is me.

HOPE FOR THE GOOD DAUGHTERS

My friend Cindi calls herself a recovering Good Daughter. Growing up, she never felt good enough, despite all her efforts. Recently she told me, "Trying hard to please God kept me from doing a lot of really bad things, but while that might sound good, I was doing it for all the wrong reasons. It just led me to utter despair because of the gross insecurity I felt inside. I believed God wouldn't—couldn't—love me because of all my faults."

It wasn't until Cindi came to grips with the sin of her self-oriented "goodness" that she started to become free.

Like Cindi, Martin Luther was a man who knew about the sin of "goodness," of *self*-righteousness. As a Catholic priest in Germany in the early 1500s, Luther diligently, desperately tried to achieve forgiveness of his sin by spending hours in prayer and in self-flagellation. Nothing he tried, however, rid him of the guilt he felt before God. Finally, he read these words in the first chapter of the book of Romans: "The just shall live by faith" (v. 17, KJV). Once he grasped that concept—that both salvation *and* living as a Christian are by grace and grace alone—he preached the radical message that Christian believers must repent of their righteousness as well as of their sin, for both are enemies of the Cross.

Centuries earlier the prophet Isaiah had said something similar when he declared, "All our righteous acts are like filthy rags" (Isaiah 64:6). Even our "goodness" is not good. *Even as Christians,* our best efforts are nothing more than grimy rags if the motivation behind our good works is to somehow earn favor with God. The fact is, we can do nothing except allow Christ's righteousness to work in and through us. Christ was the obedient elder brother who carried us across the river that separated us from the Father. It's *his* righteousness that's credited to our account. We do nothing; we can do nothing. It's all been done for us by our gracious, holy, all-mighty God.

Awesome is the word Cindi and I like to use when we talk about God. Since we're both originally from Southern California, we like to add the phrase *way cool.* God is awesome and he is way cool to have provided us with a way back to himself that takes no effort on our part. We've already contributed by sinning. *That's* our part. The rest is his because it's all about him and not about us. The Cross is his idea, his doing, his plan from start to finish, for his glory and not ours. As for the good deeds he has prepared in advance for us to do (Ephesians 2:10), they're still for God's glory.

The other day Cindi and I were talking about this very subject and musing about good deeds and Good Daughters and rewards in heaven. We concluded that while we work toward rewards in heaven, they're not going to be bigger houses closer to Jesus or furniture from Ethan Allen instead of Wal-Mart. Instead, every good thing that God gives us to do here on earth is going toward jewels in crowns that we're going to cast at the feet of Christ!

Revelation 4 describes the scene in heaven: the angels, the elders, and all the redeemed singing, "Holy, holy, holy is the Lord God Almighty, who was, and is, and is to come." Then as the worshipers lay the crowns the Lord has given them back at his feet, they sing, "You are worthy, our Lord and God, to receive glory and honor and power, for you created all things, and by your will they were created and have their being" (Revelation 4:8-11).

No striving, no competition. Not with anyone else or even within ourselves. Everything we do is simply an offering to our Lord. That's because it's not about us, and it never was. It has always been about him. Everything, from start to finish and throughout eternity, is all about the One who sits upon the throne. He is Lord, God, Almighty. He has done it all. We don't have to try to be the Good Daughter anymore. Our God has already made us Good Daughters.

That, my friend, is the gospel, and it's the gospel that will set us free.

Think on These Things

1. What are some good things that Christians do in their daily walk with the Lord? What are some reasons they might have for engaging in these activities?

2. Read Galatians 1:1-9; 3:1-5; 4:8-10; and 5:1-12. What were Paul's concerns for the Galatians? What are some ways Christians today turn to a "different" gospel? (Think of the rules some Christians live by.)

3. Martin Luther told his followers that Christians must repent of their righteousness. He also said in his Ninety-five Theses that repentance is a way of life. What is repentance? (See Psalm 51:4,17; Isaiah 57:15; Hosea 14:1-4.) How can repentance be a way of life for you?

4. Read Romans 8:1-17. What does it mean to be controlled by the Spirit (v. 9)? Memorize verses 1 and 2 or write them out and tape them someplace where you will see them daily. How do these verses help correct *self*-righteous thinking?

If I tried to fulfill the law myself, I could not trust in what I had accomplished, neither could it stand up to the judgment of God. So...I rest only upon the righteousness of Christ...which I do not produce, but receive. God the Father freely giving it to us through Jesus Christ.

—Martin Luther, *Commentary on Galatians*

Chapter 19

God Always Sends a Fish

A man's worst difficulties begin when he is able to do as he likes.
—Thomas Huxley

I've always wanted to be free. Although I'm a big coward and would never attempt this while still in my right mind, I'm fascinated with people who jump out of airplanes on purpose. Or hang glide off the cliffs over the ocean.

Where I used to live in California, people would strap odd-looking contraptions on their backs and run as fast as they could off a ramp and then, if they were fortunate, soar over the cold waters of the Monterey Bay. (The unfortunate ones would end up in the water and have to try again.) The ones who made it would catch the wind just so and sail away through the sky and down the beach. I would watch them and shake my too-sensible-to-do-*that* head but secretly wish I were the one up there flying through the clouds.

I practically grew up at the beach. When we were young, our Sunday afternoons were spent at Zuma Beach, near Malibu. We would pack the cooler with egg- or tuna-salad sandwiches wrapped in waxed paper, cans of Shasta sodas (assorted flavors), a pink box of cookies from my grandmother's bakery, and a couple bags of chips and then pile into the car and drive through Topanga Canyon and through the tunnel to Zuma. We liked Zuma Beach because it had swings and lifeguards and Italian ices at the snack bar.

When I was young, and either fearless or stupid, I liked to swim in the ocean past where the waves begin. If you can reach that spot, nothing can get you or hurt you—or so you think. However, before you get there, you have to endure waves breaking on your head and pushing you under water.

Despite the gallons of seawater that I either swallowed or inhaled, I kept trying to swim out past the waves…and I kept getting clobbered by them. You would think when a person gets knocked down constantly she would give up. Maybe a smart person would, but not a young girl, and then a young woman, with her mind set on finding freedom. I remember thinking, *If I could only reach that place where I can do whatever I want, a place where there aren't any boundaries or rules or limitations, then I could be free.* To me, the ocean represented that place: vast, huge, limitless.

The only problem was the waves. Sometimes they would rise to awesome heights, like giant walls of water keeping me away. To me they were annoying obstacles, much like the rules and regulations of my life, or the childhood catechism lessons that would haunt me, or a conscience that would attempt to spoil my fun whenever I found myself involved in something wrong. I couldn't understand why it was so difficult to get past those waves!

I remember one time being out in the water with my brother Jim. He was only seven and I was twelve. We got caught in an undertow that kept pulling us downward. I still don't know how we made it out alive, but I do remember him holding my hand and telling me not to be afraid. I should have been afraid, but instead I was mad! I wanted to get past those waves.

We made it back to shore, and instead of learning my lesson, the following Sunday I was back out there, fighting the waves and trying to get to the open water. I had this crazy notion of riding in an inner tube to Catalina Island twenty-seven miles away. Float for a year or two. At twelve, I didn't think about dangers like sharks and storms. Just about being free.

As you can probably guess, I never made it to Catalina, although I did manage a few times to get to the spot past where the waves break and the water swells. When you can get there, the feeling is indescribable. The flow of the water lifts you up, and you feel a sense of rhythm and cadence, a smooth ebb and flow, like you can stay there forever, just floating free. All you need is for someone to bring you an occasional hamburger and fries.

Unfortunately, that "freedom" moment is all too brief. The one or two times I ever reached that place, invariably I would try to find my family on the beach and, unable to spot them, realize how far I had drifted. Then I'd panic. With water too deep to touch the bottom, I'd start to cry and wish I were back on the beach digging for sand crabs with my sister.

Eventually my dad would swim out to rescue me and scold me for venturing out so far. In no uncertain terms he'd remind me of the jellyfish that sting and the kelp beds that entangle, not to mention the dangerous currents that pull even the strongest swimmers under the water. I'd promise and vow never to do it again, but...you know how it is. As soon as he turned his head, I was out there again.

It's that wanting what you don't have, or wanting to do what you're prohibited from doing, that drives you into the ocean. It's the pull of freedom's false promise that you can do as you please, make your own rules. It's not wanting to submit to authority, not wanting to obey anyone but yourself, and thinking that you know best. But it doesn't work that way. Even if you find your way to the place where you think freedom is, that place without boundaries, that's when you discover that what you thought was freedom isn't freedom at all. Instead, it's a trap that pulls you under the water, sin that tangles and ensnares. Before you know it, you're taking in water and struggling to survive.

If you're fortunate, you'll find yourself swallowed by a fish.

A FISH CALLED GRACE

The Bible says God "provided a great fish to swallow Jonah" (Jonah 1:17). First God sent the storm, which caused the men on the boat to toss Jonah overboard. Then, to keep Jonah from drowning, God sent a great fish to swallow him. In the margin of my Bible on that page I've written, "A rescue—a *good thing*."

God always sends a fish to keep his children from destruction. Sometimes it's sickness, an accident, financial trouble, a wayward child, a difficult relationship. Sometimes it's a lot of little things: a baby who refuses to sleep longer than an hour at a time, a toddler who's a picky eater, a friendship that requires a lot of attention, a car that constantly breaks down. Most of the time, as in my case, the fish is the consequence of clinging to worthless idols and the forfeiting of the grace that could be ours. It's the frustration of living a life chasing after gods of our own making, false gods who cannot satisfy. It's feeling trapped by our circumstances and bound by the wrong choices we've made. It's the resulting emptiness from the folly of thinking we can be free apart from God—be free *from* God.

So we rail against the fish, thinking it's our obstacle to freedom. But then in the midst of our fury and suffering, our anger, our guilt and shame, we hear the Lord tell us, "Fear not, for I have redeemed you; I have summoned you by name; you are mine" (Isaiah 43:1). That's when we realize that true freedom can be found even inside a fish. That as awful as the whole fish-belly experience might be, it's actually a gift of grace, a means of rescue to a drowning, wayward child. And he sends fish after fish after fish to snatch us away from danger in order that we might be truly, completely, totally free.

"Does that mean we can live any old way we want?" the apostle Paul asks. "Since we're free in the freedom of God, can we do anything that comes to mind? Hardly. You know well enough from your own experience that there are some acts of so-called freedom that destroy freedom. Offer yourselves to sin, for instance, and it's your last free act. But offer yourselves to the ways of God and the freedom never quits. All your lives you've let sin tell you what to do. But thank God you've started listening to a new master, one whose commands set you free to live openly in *his* freedom!" (Romans 6:15-18, MSG).

In our entire discussion about idols, it all comes down to this: We want to be free. We want to soar on the heights, ride the wind, free-fall through the clouds, swim, float, dance. After all, it's for freedom that Christ has set us free (Galatians 5:1).

But what does that mean? I don't know about you, but I need visual, concrete, real-life illustrations to understand things. Abstract words like *freedom* and *grace* tend to produce a glazed look on my face. I understand sin, I understand wanting to do as I please and ending up trapped as a result. I understand violating rules and reaping the consequences. I know what chains and self-made prisons and fish innards look like. But what does *freedom* look like? How would I know it in my own life? If it's not obtained by doing as I please, then how do I get it?

Now, I'm no theologian, but I have been set free. Not that I always live like I've been set free, but I'm making progress. Here's how I see freedom: The freedom we have in Christ is the freedom to (a) doubt and question, (b) fail greatly and still know we're accepted, (c) be honest with ourselves and others, (d) obey the Father out of gratitude, and (e) continuously repent and forever rejoice.

I know God's not intimidated by my doubts and questions. *Lord, how could you let that fourteen-year-old boy get gunned down on his own doorstep? Why won't you do something so my daughter and her dad will get along? I've been praying for years about the same thing—are you even listening? I'm not sure what to believe about baptism. A talking donkey in the Bible? A man being swallowed by a fish? Come on—isn't that a little far-fetched?*

I have the freedom to approach the throne with the boldness of a child going to visit her Father, who loves her dearly (Hebrews 4:16), to ask the unreasonable, to throw a tantrum without fear of being fried on the spot or banished from the kingdom. Does this mean I can come to the throne in a disrespectful, rebellious manner? Well...yes, I *can*, but I wouldn't want to. I have the freedom to rebel—nothing can separate me from God's love (Romans 8:39)—but I also have the freedom and the power to choose to behave respectfully. Just because I can do something doesn't mean I should.

Freedom allows me to doubt and question, and also to fail greatly and still know I'm accepted completely. When I examine my life, I see one of my greatest failures as the way I parent. I fiercely love my daughters, but it's not a disciplining, limit-setting love. It's more of a self-serving, I'll-be-a-really-cool-mom-so-you'll-like-me love. Unfortunately, that type of parenting produces insecure children who secretly, desperately want limits and tend to live recklessly until they find them. I feel I have failed one daughter in particular by not setting and enforcing limits from the time she was small.

However, as much as I feel I have failed, so much more has God forgiven me and has promised to work all things, including my failures, together for good (Romans 8:28) as I repent and replace my idol of wanting to be accepted with his acceptance of me. Not only that, when I do he gives me the freedom and the power to go on and do the right thing, the hard thing, standing firm in his strength and the power of his might (Ephesians 6:10). *Hallelujah!*

The freedom to fail greatly and still be accepted also means I can step out and be a complete fool for Jesus. I can stammer and fumble when I share the gospel, write books that never sell, sing off-key, and be laughed at by high school kids when I invite them to church. Being free means being okay before my Father.

Being free also means I can be honest, open, and transparent, with myself as well as with others. I don't have to sugarcoat things when I tell you of my failures and my struggles to be loved and accepted. Sometimes I lie to protect myself; I'm always tempted to cheat on my taxes. I'm not at all compassionate or generous. But I'm free, so I don't have to hide these things from you anymore and pretend I'm better than I really am.

I got a call a few years ago from a woman who was considering me as a speaker for her women's group. She asked me, "How much time do you spend in the Word every day?" I could've told her anything, then promised myself to actually put in that amount of time for a few days so I wouldn't technically be lying, but I chose instead to be free. (I wanted to tell her I didn't appreciate her question and that it was none of her business, but I'm not *that* free.) I told her the truth, that I don't spend nearly enough time in the Word. Some days I don't even open my Bible at all. Not surprisingly, I didn't hear from her again.

Frankly, I'm a mess, but I'm progressively getting better. That's because, while I'm free to be a mess and be honest about it, I'm also free to obey God with a heart full of gratitude. Free to live within the boundaries of his law. Free to not lie, not cheat, not steal, not overeat or gossip. Free to do whatever I desire. And as a believer in Christ, the One who has set me free, my greatest desire is to please God. Not that I always do the God-pleasing thing, but I want to. And I have the freedom and the power to. *Yes!*

In his book *When Being Good Isn't Good Enough,* Steve Brown writes, "What does it mean to be free in Christ? It means we are free from the rules we thought bound us to God. It means we are free from the manipulation other Christians use to make us like them—free from having to fit into the world's mold, free to be different. We are free from the slavery of religion and from the fear of rejection, alienation and guilt. We are free from the fear of death. We are free from masks, free from the sham and pretense; free to doubt, free to risk, free to question. It means we are free to live every moment. But most of all, we are free to follow Christ, not because we have to but because we want to."[1]

It is for freedom that we have been set free, to doubt and question, to fail and still be accepted, to be honest, to obey, and to live a life of continuous repentance and subsequent rejoicing. God sends fish into our lives to swallow us that we might repent, to repent that we might rejoice.

From inside the fish Jonah prayed. In his distress he called to the Lord and acknowledged, "You hurled me into the deep…all your waves and breakers swept over me. I said, 'I have been banished from your sight; yet I will look again toward your holy temple'" (Jonah 2:3-4). He repented and rejoiced. While still inside the fish, he rejoiced!

When I was young, I was foolishly fearless of the waves that crashed on top of me. As an adult, I'm actually afraid of them. I have a troubling, recurring dream of a tsunami-proportion wave rising up out of nowhere. Just as it crests and is about to send certain death my way, I'm scooped up and placed inside a container, like a clear, Plexiglas box. At first I'm terrified, especially as I watch the wave crash over me. I can see the water swirling violently around me, and sometimes I'm thrown about the container. In one version of the dream the box fills up with water, but it never reaches the top. In these "wave dreams" as I call them, I'm never consumed by the water. As everything is demolished around me, I am saved.

Out in the water, I'm destroyed, but inside that confining container, inside the confines of the law of God and the boundaries set by his love, inside the fish placed there by his grace, I'm *free*. Free to find my self-image in him, free to feast at his table. Free to put off busyness and be still before him, and to be content with what his hand provides. Free to know him and be known by him, to be real and kind, to trust his plans for my life, and to love others from the overflow of his love for me. I'm free to fail and to have no one applaud me but him, to find joy in submission, sweetness in his love. I'm free to be dependent on others…and to forgive.

I'm free to lift up holy hands in heartfelt gratitude, to whisper in humble adoration, to laugh and cry tears of joy, to shout with jubilant praise. I'm free to open my fists to surrender my idols because I'm loved and accepted, forgiven and redeemed, adopted by the King…because I've been set free.

Notes

Chapter 1

1. Timothy Keller, from a study on Galatians soon to be published by Redeemer Presbyterian Church, New York, NY.

Chapter 4

1. John Ortberg, "Taking Care of Busyness," *Leadership Journal* (fall 1998).

Chapter 8

1. Carol Kent, *Tame Your Fears* (Colorado Springs, Colo.: NavPress, 1993), 72-4.

Chapter 9

1. Nancy Kennedy, *Help! I'm Being Intimidated by the Proverbs 31 Woman!* (Sisters, Oreg.: Multnomah, 1995), 161.

Chapter 13

1. Louis A. Tartaglia, M.D., *Flawless!* (New York: Eagle Brook, 1999), 12-3.

Chapter 15

1. Judith Viorst, *I'll Fix Anthony* (New York: Simon & Schuster, 1969).

Chapter 18

1. Max Lucado, *In the Grip of Grace* (Nashville: Word, 1996), 1.

Chapter 19

1. Steve Brown, *When Being Good Isn't Good Enough* (Grand Rapids: Baker, 1990), 66.

About the Author

Nancy Kennedy has written professionally since 1989. Her work has appeared in such publications as *Christian Parenting, Marriage Partnership, Virtue, Today's Christian Woman, Aspire,* and many other national magazines and newspapers. Her books include *Help! I'm Being Intimidated by the Proverbs 31 Woman; Mom on the Run;* and *Honey, They're Playing Our Song* (Multnomah); and *Prayers God Always Answers* (WaterBrook Press).

Nancy also works as a staff reporter for the *Citrus County Chronicle,* where her weekly religion page feature story has won two First Place Excellence in Religion Feature Writing awards from the Florida Press Club. In addition to writing, she speaks to women's groups on the subject of living free in Christ. She is the mother of two daughters, is married to Barry, and lives in Inverness, Florida.

Nancy can be contacted at:
Nancy Kennedy
c/o Seven Rivers Presbyterian Church
4221 W. Gulf-to-Lake Hwy.
Lecanto, FL 34461